THE MANY COLORED BUFFALO

Transformation Through The Council of Voices

FRONTIERS IN PSYCHOTHERAPY SERIES

Edward Tick, *Series Editor*

The Many Colored Buffalo, by William S. Taegel

in preparation

Freud & Cezanne: Psychotherapy as Modern Art, *by Alexander Jasnow*

Hope Under Seige: State Terror vs. Family Support in Chile, *by Michelle Ritterman*

My Father was Shiva, *by James Flosdorf*

Relational Psychotherapy in Practice, *by Robert Willis*

What to Do Until Enlightenment, *by Stuart Alpert*

THE MANY COLORED BUFFALO

Transformation Through The Council of Voices

Dr. William S. Taegel

The Center for Creative Resources, Inc.
Creative Family Resources, Inc.
Houston, TX

Printed in the United States of America

Library of Congress Cataloging-in-Publication Data

Taegel, William S., 1940-
The many colored buffalo : transformation through the council of voices / by William S. Taegel.
p. cm. — (Frontiers in psychotherapy)
Includes bibliographical references and index.
ISBN 0-89391-739-7. — ISBN 0-89391-740-0 (pbk.)
1. Psychotherapy. 2. Self. I. Title. II. Series.
RC489.S43T34 1990
616.89'14—dc20 90-46541
CIP

Ablex Publishing Corporation
355 Chestnut Street
Norwood, New Jersey 07648

This book is for my partner on the path,
Judith L. Yost

Table of Contents

About the Author

William Taegel is in the private practice of psychotherapy, as well as co-director—with his wife Judith L. Yost, MSW—of the Center for Creative Resources in Houston. Having earned a doctorate in psychotherapy and religion, he continues to explore that interest in this book. He also is associate editor of *Voices: The Journal of the American Academy of Psychotherapists.* As a naturalist he teaches extensively in the Continental Medicine Wheel and other shamanic settings.

Series Introduction to *The Many Colored Buffalo*

Edward Tick, Ph.D., Series Editor

I am pleased and proud to present William Taegel's *The Many Colored Buffalo* as the first volume in *The Frontiers of Psychotherapy* book series. While there exist several excellent volumes that focus exclusively on Native American and Shamanic healing traditions, and a few books of psychiatric and psychological exploration of those traditions, Dr. Taegel's book and methodology presents the first full integration of Native American shamanic healing with psychodynamic psychotherapy.

William Taegel is well suited for such an undertaking. Born and raised in the rugged terrain of western Texas, he had early exposure to Native American ways and teachings. But, perhaps more fundamentally, it was the earth itself that was Taegel's first teacher. These early teachers were left behind for a while, returning to guide and serve Taegel only after he had explored the limits of traditional psychotherapy.

After full training and a busy career in the mental health field, one that rightly included much personal psychotherapy, Taegel took the bold step of entering shamanic training and initiation with Native American medicine people in the Komatsi, Creek, and other traditions. He was seeking to awaken and heal parts of himself that were both deeply wounded and buried and also so basic to our animal nature that they were inaccessible indoors. So Taegel took first his personal search and then his practice into the wilderness.

Taegel's personal journey and those of his clients and his practice offer a perspective that important teachers, including Lao Tzu, St. Francis, and Chief Seattle in past times and Gregory Bateson, R.D. Laing, and Alan Watts in our own, have offered. It is that the way to healing our neuroses, our malaise, and anomie and discontent, is in returning to the earth, awakening to and healing our relationship to the natural order, reclaiming our primitive and animalistic feelings, needs, drives, and urges, broadening our personalities that have become cut off and deadened due to over-socialization.

In the consulting room through an expansion of expressive therapy techniques guided by the therapist's broadening awareness, in the larger therapy office of the Native American Inipi, sweatlodge, and hamblecheyapi, vision quest, and in the largest office of all, the wilderness, William Taegel offers means for awakening and accessing the numerous energies and forces that make up the full human being. Due to personal wounding as well as life in modern civilization, many of these energies will have soured or taken distorted pathways for expression. But with the guidance of a vision of human living that achieves fullness only when reconnected to the natural world and with indoor and outdoor techniques for accessing, cleansing, and expressing those energies, they may be regained and the individual reconnected to self, other, community, and planet.

R.D. Laing has warned that we have become so used to our present dis-eased and fallen condition that we accept it as normal. The challenge today is to reject our so-called normalcy and rediscover lost connections, energies, and parts of ourselves that are parts of nature as well and that include the darkness as well as light. Much more health and well-being are possible than we quite know how to imagine in our present condition. William Taegel's courageous and innovative theories and exploration, integrating one of the most honored ancient traditions with contemporary psychotherapy and living, take us a long way toward that ancient and new vision of the full human being at home on a living planet that loves us as her true children.

Preface

After first perusing the manuscript of this book, my editor suggested that I read James Lovelock's hypothesis that the Earth is a coherent system of life. He saw us as having similar views of that possibility. To my delight I discovered a scientist who postulates the Earth as self-regulating and self-changing, an immense living organism, a single physiological entity. He called this notion the *Gaia hypothesis,* Gaia being the Greek goddess Earth. The two of us started from radically different places: he as a British scientist on loan to NASA in Houston, and I as a psychotherapist in private practice in that same city.

In his work as a space scientist, he first beheld the Earth as a whole from the perspective of outerspace and his hypothesis burst forth, as if out of the future. Restless with the limitations of traditional psychotherapy, I returned to my personal past in the Llano Estacado of Texas that led me to gaze through the clear eyes of Native American shamans. Eventually, I found a third eye to see not only the Earth but the Universe as a manifestation of a single Being, a constellation of parts and subparts, energy flows where everything relates. Only a few blocks away from each other, Lovelock and I labored in a similar vineyard but never met.

These were the early 1970s, and I was shy about my experiments, so much so that I talked to few people about the results of my own inner lab. During this period of gestation, I found that Native Americans not only listened but also greatly stimulated my work. These discussions were not on an intellectual plane, but lead me directly into the world of Nature where shamans live and work: the cliffs of Kaui, the rain forests of Central America, the high deserts of New Mexico and Oregon, and the awesome variety of terrain in Texas, to mention a few.

I want to acknowledge these many sources of wisdom from the world of the shaman: O-nee-ha, the O-Piv/Quena Lodge, the Thunder Lodge, the Chi-Sho-Gi Lodge, the Seattle Lodge, and other informal medicine societies that have included the Navajo, the Delaware, the Cherokee, the Lakota, the Komatsi, the Apache, the Creek, and many others. To Marc Bearheart I offer special thanks for our time of walking the pathway together; in our agreements and disagreements I learned much. His reflections can be seen especially in the early chapters. Recently, the Alabama-Coushatta, my gentle but proud neighbors a few small towns to the north, have allowed me to draw nourishment from their woods, sleep on their grounds, and drink their spring water as I let go of this book.

All these original North Americans have shared with me their campfires and their souls. Through the millenia they tuned themselves into unseen flows of energy and used the assumption that human beings moved from balance to imbalance and then a return to balance through a purifying and visionary experience that resulted in new awareness.

This process of balance, imbalance, jolt of new energy, and movement to a new level of balance through awareness I came to call "transformation."

The book offers a narration of experiences, events, and observations about this process. It is to be read as a myth; it is not an attempt in any way to reveal objective or historical truth, generally or specifically. Once a shaman told me about traveling to South America on a beam of light to talk with a fellow shaman. I asked him if it really happened or if he was just offering a teaching tale. He laughed and laughed and asked me if what we had seen on the evening news that night on television really happened or was it just a teaching tale?

Along this line all characters in the "case" studies are composites and do not refer to any one individual. Creatively, this approach fits my purposes best, and in this way the identities of clients are also protected. I want to thank all my clients, colleagues, and students who have encouraged me along this path of transformation. Many could care less about ancient myths and shamanism, but they have taught me much by drawing into my awareness parts of myself that I would never have known were it not for the difficult places we have walked together. They, whether they knew it or not, forced me to the frontiers to explore the boundaries.

In the world of psychotherapy, I am grateful to Hal Stone and Sidra Winkleman, explorers of the terrain of the psychology of selves; Jay

Maxwell, thinker and guide in psychodynamics; an ongoing group of psychotherapists who have held my feet to the fire for over a decade; all those of a ecosystemic bias; and Mike Mauldin, partner at the Center for Creative Resources in Houston.

Ed Tick, my editor, fits all the categories of psychotherapist, shaman, and writer; he has provided encouragement and expertise in ways that have made the book possible and that have provoked me into dimensions of exploration that lead even now beyond this endeavor.

To a trio of women—Juanita, my mother, and Kris and Holly, daughters—I offer thanks for being supportive and making allowances for my talks with nonhuman creatures, sweat lodges, and visions quests. Though they sometimes thought my experiments idiosyncratic, they almost always respected my right to journey into dimensions I held as important.

Finally, I thank Judith Yost, partner in pursuit of awareness, who believed in this book when its supporters were few and in her mate when his courage was low.

Just before I mailed this manuscript to the publisher I had a dream. In this dream people were driving up and down a freeway, and I was in a large building that had glass walls. It was a wonderful building that appeared as a NBA sports arena. As the people drove by on the freeway, they turned to look into the building, where I talked to a group about significant matters. I felt vulnerable, scared, overexposed, and wondered about the people on the freeway that I didn't know. Then, after a while, I accustomed myself to the traffic and even enjoyed it. It was as if the cars would actually come into the arena, although I didn't know how they could do that.

In the time that followed, I viewed the dream as a commentary on you, the readers, looking into my world, even joining it for our mutual exploration. At least this is the hope that comes from my inner world.

William Taegel
Houston, 1990

Introduction

Long before sunrise a tow-headed boy of six opened his eyes and with the backs of his hands, pawed away the sleep in his eyes. Today was Saturday, no school. For one short day he would be free of the hated constriction of sitting in a classroom, bolted away by heavy doors from trees he loved to climb, clods he loved to throw, and butterflies he loved to watch.

Just as first light cast an orange glow on the late fall day, he and his father left their truck, the man carrying a shotgun for bird hunting. To his right, twisting and darting, a small spring-fed creek, the Prairie Dog Fork of the Red River, continued its ageless job of cutting a gorge, now seven hundred feet deep and a mile across at the point where boy and father squatted to tie their shoes.

Across the water a herd of pronghorn antelope munched along, headed by a proud buck with alert ears. To his left rose the canyon's south wall, whose colors flashed reds, blues, burnt oranges and whites, like the skirts of Spanish dancers after whom it was named. Along the canyon floor the summer grass had turned brown, as had the stubby mesquite. The yucca remained green, while next to the water the usually squat juniper thrived and reached up some forty feet into the sky.

The boy didn't have a gun to hunt quail, so he sat at the base of a towering cottonwood tree and nibbled a biscuit his mother had packed for him, while his father and his friends listened for the sound of bobwhite wings. Finished with his breakfast, the boy practiced the sound of quail wings by blowing air through his lips. He followed a trail to his left, going up the little river for a short distance and then climbing the left shoulder of the canyon toward an opening he could see from below. Holding onto the roots of the junipers, he pulled himself up until at last he reached his destination.

Little did he know it also was his destiny.

The direction of his life would pass before him in the next hour, or was it two. How much was fact, how much fiction?

The opening in the canyon wall turned out to be a shallow cave carved by the river at another time. Its floor was lined with a powder that crept over the top of his tennis shoes to leave grit as reminders of where he had been. Its ceiling, red and rich. The morning light did not reach the back wall, and the boy, shy of the dark, did not venture beyond the light. Bones with traces of meat and hair lay in the shadows within an arm's reach of where he sat.

Although another creature lived there, the boy felt at home, as if he had been there before and sat beneath the overhang of the cave's mouth looking across to the North wall. Off to the right stretched the ever-widening canyon that meandered across the Texas landscape for hundreds of unpeopled miles.

To his left and down on the canyon floor, towered a large stand of cottonwood, their leaves showing their white bellies and changing colors as they responded to the gentle urge of the first winds of a Canadian norther. Against the pink-ribbed clouds that reached across the clearing, the boy spotted a moving dot.

The dot sliced downward, becoming larger as it hurtled ever closer. Squinting his eyes and using his hand as a visor, he soon could hear the speeding bird's wings harp in the wind. The wings drew into a delta, and the boy whistled to himself at the speed he guessed at over a hundred miles per hour, maybe two hundred.

Flapping up the canyon from the west came a familiar owl, known as the night eagle to the Komatsi and Kiowa who had made this canyon their sacred home through the millenia. Unaware of the speeding delta of the larger burnished brown bird hurtling toward it, the owl, its heart-shaped face looking peaceful, continued its journey.

By now the boy could see that the wings of the large bird reached across seven feet or more. No doubt remained: it was a golden eagle. It looked like it would grab the owl with its talons, but instead it made fists of its talons and punched the speeding owl at the base of its right wing.

For a moment, an eternal moment that would play hide and seek with his consciousness for the rest of the boy's life, the eagle and the owl rolled in a struggle for air space. As feathers flew, death waited nearby.

Soon the owl, no small bird itself, dropped like a rock to the ground, then lurched into the thick limbs of the juniper that the boy had used as a hand-hold, safe by just a whisker from another savage punch that would have been fatal.

But, wounded as it was, could it survive?

Fascinated and horrified, the boy's sympathies stretched between these two guardians of sky. The night eagle roamed free in the dark while the golden eagles, tericel and hen, ruled the day. It was this time between night and day where tension and conflict erupted onto a field of honor. Who owned this time?

The cry and the hoot competed for the boy's ear, and he could feel something being pulled out of his inner depths; a tension from within resonated with the conflict in the sky; powerful feelings rose in his spindly breast, one gentle and one rageful, pulling at one another.

This primal scene came to the boy of my childhood in the Palo Duro Canyon, called by the Komatsi and Kiowa the "canyon of the hard wood." I would learn many things in my life, but all of what I would need for wisdom was there that morning. It would need to ferment in my unconscious for nearly half a century before it bubbled to the top of my consciousness as a guide, but it was there in embryonic form.

This book probes the tension of these inner forces of night and day, the selves that compete for our attention, and the possibility of transformation in this tension so graphically depicted by the owl and the eagle. It describes a process of learning to listen to these selves in a different way through Native myths and ceremonies, through shamanic activities, and through a variety of therapeutic modes that promote expression. It also describes the possibility of the synergy of these healing traditions in an effort to recover the natural balance of the person in relationship to the planetary environment.

When people come to me for psychotherapy, a workshop, or some other form of learning, they generally sense a gnawing pain somewhere inside. Long before we get to the pain in any depth, they present aspects of themselves that want to know how safe it is to work with me. They want to know how long it is going to take, how much it is going to cost, whether I am firm enough to handle some aspects that yearn to be expressed, and whether I will hurt them by being critical, punitive, and perfectionistic. At some level of their being, they wonder, mostly through energies hidden from their conscious mind, if I am trapped by my own skin or if I have points of contact within, open to Something More.

Yet they are also leery of a process that seeks to please their every whim and desire; they have too much of that already through a consumer society. Although it may not be apparent to them at the time, they seek safety from rampant desires without entirely blocking these impulses. On the one hand they are terrified of the deeper contours of energy in themselves and the universe, but, on the other hand, they experience a drying up of the fresh spring waters that fed them when they entered the planet. They want to know if there is a way to tap into these deeper flows of energy without being destroyed by them. They want to know if I am flexible enough to work with what is unique to them and, at the same time, know a pathway to which I can point and offer guidance.

They want to know if I will trap them and not let them go when it is time, if I will express myself to them but not overwhelm them, and if I will offer guidance rather than passivity. Some of these questions cannot be answered easily and will take time.

What they hear in the beginning are vibrating hints about my own unfolding transformation. These energetic hints of a personal saga where wayward voices broke out of my inner cellar to cause me difficulties were prophesied by the eagle and the owl. They do not want to know the details of my story, but they do want to be able to sense a vibration that tells them I listen to inner selves that trouble me. As I listen to them, I also listen to aspects of myself that may vibrate as they talk. Eventually, they will know if I can tap into flows of energy that arise in me as they talk and act. They will know it by the exchange of energy between us.

As I write, I also invite the reader into a similar field of energy. I am committed to transactions where I bring awareness of my own various energies to the table. I aim at not writing or transacting outside the field of my own personal experience unless I acknowledge that I am beyond myself. Only in this way can I stand behind my work in therapy and the markings of this book.

Yet, even in a book where I go over the writing many times, I cannot guarantee that this aim of awareness is always there. In even the most evolved people on the planet, awareness is present in a given day only a small portion of the time. At any moment I can be dominated by a subunit of energy from my unconscious that blots out my awareness.

At moments that you sense my departure from my own awareness of myself and my environment in this book, I invite your confrontation. I also invite confrontation of other disagreements with points of view that have in them the substance of awareness. The way you and I interlock energies with the world and each other has important distinctions, and it is in these distinctions that we can learn from each other. So I invite you to allow your various energies to rage against or applaud, so that we have a living conversation and mutual voicing of our inner energies.

My clients and I don't have this class of encounter all the time; sometimes, we just pass the time through dry passages. Occasionally, we meet in a mutual voicing. When we do, the energy of transformation is there. I hope these quality moments will occur from time to time in this book and pull out hidden voices from within.

When I was a boy of seven, I experienced the eruption of a hidden voice, a year after I saw the fight between the eagle and the owl. I was so troubled by the stress of a dysfunctioning family that I chopped down an entire garden of corn I had carefully cultivated over a summer. This rageful act was clearly directed toward the larger family and cultural system, but it came seemingly out of nowhere. All the time I chopped, a hoarse voice screamed in a tone that was foreign to my ears.

After the rage was spent, I sat in the middle of the felled corn and cried, awash in confusion about where the rage and the behavior had originated. This rageful voice was followed quickly by shame and remorse as I sobbed over my own loss and the destruction of the plants I had cultivated and loved.

All summer I had lovingly tended those beloved plants. They were my best friends, yet something inside burst through a door and took over my actions. Where had the rage originated? It seemed deeper than just anger at my family of origin. Was it directed at the process of being tamed? Was it connected with the summer ending and being forced indoors? Was this the conflict of eagle and owl?

Early on, people who work with me in the therapy process notice a hypothesis that grows out of the above experience and others like it. The hypothesis holds that broken personal relationships are projected onto the natural environment, and, just as important, abuse of the natural environment ultimately deteriorates the intimate environment. It is the shaman who can guide us in the natural environment, and the psychotherapist who helps us navigate the psychodynamic and interpersonal environment.

I personally have tried many approaches with these myriad voices within. I have tried the iron fist of will power to silence certain troublesome ones. I have tried various religious ceremonies to purge myself of energies that seem toxic. I have sought analysts, various therapists, body workers, and spiritual teachers who have led me toward insight. I have attended twelve-step programs and a variety of group therapy processes. In these various ways I have harbored the mistaken notion that, somehow, I can get rid of certain troublesome voices, voices that have haunted me for as long as I can remember, voices like the one that destroyed the corn plants.

One approach told me to analyze the underlying conflicts, and that, by recognizing with insight the ambivalence in any situation, I would be freed of the voice. Another told me to pour out the rage in a catharsis, and I would be rid of it. Another told me to turn it over to God, and it would go away. None of these approaches was wrong, but they did not work for me. Everywhere I went, there were several "I's" following me around, including the enraged one. I could not escape from my many parts within. I could repress them, but eventually they would bob up to the surface again.

As an adult I discovered I have a scared little boy inside who trembles when someone important withdraws emotionally. In all of the ways that I mentioned—and many more—I have sought to "do" something with him. Really, I have wished that I could put him permanently away. Most of the therapies and transforming pathways have colluded with me to get rid of him as well. They don't like fear any better than anger.

Some have said I could forgive him, and he would go away. Others have said I could gain insight, and he would go away. Others have invited me to have a catharsis, as with the anger, and he would be out of my system. Others have encouraged a positive, loving approach that wanted me to ignore his tantrums when he was hurt, as in the chopping down of the corn patch.

None of these approaches was wrong, but, again, they did not work. No matter what I did, he lurched into my consciousness just at the time I didn't want him to. Mostly, he acted up in important relationships. I could hide him professionally. For long periods of time, I could "control" him so that the outside world could only see my poker face, but he was there anyway. The perceptive could sense his energy peeking out from behind my protection and control.

Once, when I was on a vision quest (I will tell you more about this process later!), this hurt little boy ventured out to speak to me, as he had on any number of occasions. This time, however, there was something inside me that could listen to him with a high quality of awareness. For a solid year after that, I spent much of my spare time listening to him—not attempting to get him to leave or feel better or anything—just listening. As I listened, I learned what he had to say. I experienced what it felt like to be in his shoes. The more I listened, the more he became convinced that I, at last, was not going to send him away. Somewhere in that process, I gave up on the possibility of having relationships where he was not present in an important way; this includes my work as a psychotherapist.

When I heard his voice during this quest, it was not the first time that he had spoken or that I had listened to him. The difference was that I was in a different state of mind, one where my awareness had been greatly heightened by the vision quest experience. In this listening process I learned that the energetic state that I have when he speaks is crucial. If I am in an angry or critical energy state when he speaks, then depression and despair are soon to follow. If I am in an aware state of energy, then a sense of warmth and nurture gradually develop.

I will tell you more about him and his close friends inside me as we go along. It is enough now to inform you that learning to listen to him and others like him is the basis of my work. These conversations constitute the inner council of voices. This reality becomes evident to my clients and students, some early in the process, some later. The overview that I present to those beginning with me is essentially a process for learning how to take care of him and his friends.

As a reader, you also deserve a brief framework for the book so you will know how much to open yourselves to its teachings. Much of the book uses myth, ceremonies, psychotherapy cases, and other metaphorical story forms to convey the process of transforming the person. These storylike forms appeal to certain inner aspects, especially the hidden ones, the childlike ones, and the primitive ones.

A first assumption of the book is that we are many selves and that these selves need to be addressed directly, even as I am doing now. I refer in part also to a process called voice vialogue, an approach taught by Hal Stone and Sidra Winkleman (1985), where the person directly engages inner aspects (or voices) in a dialogue.

Or maybe a seeker comes to me after having heard of my work with Native American ways; they would be introduced to the notion that Nature Itself pulls out the different selves from the hinterlands of our being, so that we can see them, take care of them, and eventually make better choices about how to live in partnership with our Natural environment. When there is a rupture in our relationship with the Natural world, then disruptions in our intimate environment are soon to follow, and vice versa. In my earlier example, my rage at the malfunctioning of my extended family drove me to destroy the corn plants I loved. The reverse is also true; hardening ourselves by the destruction of our natural resources eventually leads to the destruction of our intimate environment.

Either way, I employ a number of expressive therapies like voice dialogue,psychodrama, art therapy, music therapy, Gestalt therapy, Jungian analysis, free association, family therapy and psychosynthesis, hypnosis, and others. I will direct our attention to a larger psychology of selves in relationship to environment. Specific interventions will be illustrative of the transforming process and are not meant to be a clinical manual.

Further, the book is meant to be more a provoker of a shift in reality than a set of instructions about how to run your life. For one thing, I don't know what you should do with your life in a specific situation; it is a struggle for me to know that for myself. Rather, the spirit of the book is to facilitate awareness; it is meant to be something like a rooster that sits high on a fence and at the right time jumps down into the chicken coop to stir things up. After he stirs things up, he returns to his perch to observe the process he has stirred up. Through this stirring of awareness, I aim at further opening a pathway between the conscious and unconscious, thus making more data available from the various voices for better choices for you in your life.

A further assumption of this book is that we can better listen to ourselves when we listen to the natural world around us. Restoring ourselves to the wild aspects of Nature provides a context for listening to the inner, wild aspects of ourselves. The clue to balancing ourselves is in noticing with awareness the balancing in Nature.

The kind of psychotherapy that leaves the client indoors cannot reach the level of transformation that I reach for in this book. Indoor psychotherapy can pave the way and introduce movement along the spiral of transformation, but the way of transformation leads eventually to the wild and outdoors.

The natural environment seeks to teach us the absolute essential of transformation: all that exists is an energy system. Every living being is composed of a system of energy fields which interact with each other and the larger environment.

The Lakota describe the Energy Field as the Sacred Mystery *(Wakan Tanka),* a Living Being Whose backbones are the mountains and Whose bloodveins are the rivers and streams. A human being, according to the American Indian tribal ways, can best be thought of as a localization or concentration of this Universal Field of Energy. This view of the world is a basic building block for the shaman.

What, you may ask, is a shaman? In the context of this book a *shaman* is a teacher/healer who facilitates the person in moving beyond the reality of their usual resources and energies into the nonordinary reality of their hidden resources and energies. As we proceed, I will expand the meaning of the word "shaman" as a description that best portrays the person who facilitates the transforming process after the process reaches a certain depth. The shaman assumes that a person's personal energy field is composed of subfields which are interrelated and affect each other; it is to these subfields of energy (variously called *subpersonalities, aspects, parts, energy flows*) that we will direct much of our attention.

The ceremonial component of life is also examined as being important on this transformational pathway. In this book I use a sampling of Native American ceremonies like the Sweat Lodge and the Vision Quest as vehicles for exploring the transforming of ourselves. One of the ceremonial myths, to be detailed in Chapter 6, tells of a buffalo that changes its colors as a way of teaching the Lakota tribe about its own evolution. Each color suggests a dimension of the transforming process, and this metaphor will permeate this writing.

We need approaches to life that offer ceremonies that will call forth the inner voices that have been viciously cut off from the Earth. That day when I was seven years old, I literally chopped off connections between my ego and the growth of the Earth. Only when I returned to Native American ceremonies that are rooted in Nature could I begin to hear voices that were sent into exile after they were cut off from the fertility of their Mother, the Earth. Maybe it will fit for you to explore Native American ceremonies, or maybe you will explore other rituals that honor the Primitive Mystery of Earth and Sky. The test of the efficacy of a ceremony lies in its ability to draw forth as many voices as is possible for the awareness of the ego.

But before I venture too far into the ceremonial and into the storytelling needed to reach the deeper voices within, I offer a linear statement for use by the part of the conscious mind that looks for structure in order to gain safety and organization. It needs to be acknowledged at the outset so it will allow us into the secret pathways of the unconscious:

1. We will touch briefly on the notion of many selves within and assume that the person is a conglomerate of subenergy systems that interact with larger energy systems.
2. We will entertain the experience of subpersonalities, these aspects of human beings that constantly seek expression.
3. We will spend time with hunter selves that help us begin the observing process so necessary to our transformation.
4. We will begin to smoke out hidden subpersonalities in the unconscious that can enrich our identities.
5. We will then be able to vision ourselves in a different way, so that our actual identity changes.
6. All of the above paves the way for us to listen to deeply wounded subpersonalities, usually the inner children that dwell in the unconscious. These little ones provide the fuel for the transforming journey.
7. This seventh part of the outline suggests the possibility of a Higher Intelligence, a Higher Energy behind the transforming process.

Underlying the book is the assumption that access to this Higher Power comes through connecting the human organism to the Natural Order of Earth and Sky.

8. Throughout we will look at the role of the facilitator of the transformation process in the form of psychotherapist and/or shaman.

Now, having addressed some of the aspects of the reader that like outlines, I move on to tell some stories and offer some reflections to other parts of you that are open to the images of desert terrain, many colored buffaloes, a jumping mouse, and soaring eagles.

REFERENCE

Stone, H., & Winkelman, S. (1985). *Embracing ourselves.* Marina del Rey, CA: Devorss.

1

The Many Selves

An aging red-and-white Dodge pickup truck sputters along the Interstate. It crosses the Rio Grande River west of Albuquerque, swollen with heavy spring thaw, and heads toward the mesas that stretch westward to Mt. Taylor, a holy spot the local Native Americans call Turquoise, sometimes Tongue, Mountain.

Soon my companion and I leave the Interstate and take a two-lane road that devolves from paved to dirt to sand. Bouncing on old shock absorbers, we wind for miles until little trace of civilization remains.

At last, we slide to a stop.

Neither of us speak, content to absorb the scenery, replenishing ourselves after weeks in the city. The arroyos, cactus, sunburned grass, mesquite, and jackrabbits converge into what appears to be an uninhabited wasteland. Upon closer look I notice a few Navaho hogans, dust specks on the horizon.

My friend, a man in his late sixties, is a Creek Indian. Medium in height and solidly built, he sports western boots, neatly pressed Levis, a cotton shirt with Indian designs, and a large western hat. Across the front of the hat dangles a silver eagle, and from the hat band protrudes a dark feather with a yellow splash at its apex.

To restore myself from the rigors of my practice of psychotherapy, I spend as much time as possible outdoors. Marc, a medicine man with his people, is a longtime hiking companion, or at least its symbolic equivalent in the Native American Way. Another master of symbols,

Freud, was once asked if his cigar had symbolic meaning, say, as a penis. His famous reply was, "Sometimes a cigar is just a cigar." With Indian teachers the opposite is true; a hike is rarely just a hike. The symbolic meaning of our walking reaches forth with gentle hands through the physical movement as I connect with the desert around us; the movement and the desert combine to heighten my awareness.

The route to the top of the mesa twists and turns, first in soft sand and then in crumbling rock. Near the top we stop and squat, then sit crosslegged, gazing with awe at the hundreds of miles of desert outlined by distant snow-tipped mountains, the Sangre de Cristos.

As we are wont to do, our conversation turns to matters of personal growth, and my companion asks about what kind of problems prompt people to work with me in psychotherapy and various seminars. He is curious but also cautious about how psychotherapists might work with people as contrasted with his shamanic ways. His fingers have been burned by people from my culture who automatically assume that their ways are better than his. I have not escaped this ethnic arrogance: I struggle with trusting him enough to enter his world because I have been taught that newer is better and that older is less scientific, and therefore less true.

CROSSING THE INVISIBLE LINE

As I look at his dark features and consider his questions, I think of an invisible line that divides professional inquiry and existential involvement on the part of the researcher. For years I have read the publications of Mircea Eliade (1964), whose works on shamanism are the beginning point for those in our culture who want to understand the ancient healing ways. Yet Eliade did not ever cross the invisible line separating scholarly inquiry from passionate involvement.

Eliade did not experiment with the ways of the shaman to see if they might have merit in his own life and work other than as a topic of research. He did not journey into the underworld or to the upperworld to see if the energetic dimensions described to him by various shamans were actually available and relevant in a personal way for his own transformation.

Joseph Campbell (1969), the mythologist, also comes to mind in this regard. He crossed briefly over the line that separates academic inquiry from personal reality in his later years at Esalen. He participated in a rich discussion on PBS television where he came tantalizingly close to revealing his own personal transformational journey, but the personal glimpses we received were few.

As I ponder Marc, I know why historically this line has been crossed by so few: The cost is great, and the terrain is forbidding. One must, for the moment, put away the arrogance of our culture and walk in a sphere of reality where our usual ways of thinking do not prevail. The anthropologists Castaneda (1968) and Harner (1982) crossed it, as have a few psychotherapists like Carl Jung (1933), but the explorers are still few.

The reason I sit with my companion on the hillside is an intense curiosity and my sense of richness in his tradition. With him from time to time, and with several others in a medicine circle in another setting, I have decided to enter a mutual learning experience. For me, it will entail crossing this line and learning the ways of the shaman from the inside out.

For them, it will mean opening themselves to the domain of the psychotherapist. Early on, they made it clear that we could not proceed unless I was willing to challenge my personal assumptions about reality. The only way I could share in their shamanism was to cross this invisible line that separates the two cultures.

This line also provides a boundary that our culture as a whole crossed from the opposite direction at some point in the past. When we crossed, we moved away from our connections with Nature in an attempt to flee from superstition and myth into the arms of our beloved scientific method. We began to see Nature as something we had to conquer and overcome, rather than experiencing ourselves as a co-operative element in the larger Tapestry. Our fleeing from Nature led us to the brink of destroying the planet Earth as a human environment. Now in this time many of us come, hat in hand, shuffling up to the line. Paradoxically, it is the scientific method which allows us the latitude to experiment with new connections in these ancient ways.

Marc says nothing as I sit in the quiet, pondering whether to venture across this line again deeper into shamanistic territory. I have done it before, but I am cautious. This caution is not because I do not trust Marc, but because I don't know if I have enough courage to expose my work to the light of another tradition, one that is ten thousand years older than the earliest tales of European cultures.

Eventually, clear images of my psychotherapy practice appear to me as a tiny rock just to the left of my foot seems to pull the words out of my mouth. This induction reaches beyond the usual control that I exhibit in the city where I live and is typical of experience when I enter shamanic energy. The experience of the rock is shamanic, and the case that flows forward is that of the psychotherapist.

A COUPLE AND THEIR MANY SELVES

"A couple came to me a number of years ago, showing considerable pain on their faces," I began. "They obviously loved each other but were royally confused.

"What prompted their coming happened at a party they had attended months before: The woman danced with a friend of the man's, a not unusual occurrence generally handled with ease by the two of them. This time, the man explained to me, was different because the man felt intense waves of jealousy and rage roar into his consciousness, feelings that surprised and confused him because he thought of himself as reasonable and well controlled.

"The woman, Betty I'll call her, received a call from her dance partner the next day, and, to her total surprise, found herself agreeing to meet him for lunch. Later she lied to her mother and best friend about the meeting. A sexually alive and adventuresome woman of about twenty-two seemed to take over her forty-two-year-old body and 'make' her do things she wouldn't ordinarily do. After the trysts with her new-found lover, her romantic feelings would disappear, and in their place came enormous waves of judgement and criticism of herself, followed quickly by remorse, then anxiety, and finally genuine disbelief that she would risk everything to be with this man, a person completely opposite of both her husband and herself.

"At times, she realized that she wasn't in love with this man, but some energy inside seemed to break loose and drive her. This part of her seemed to tell her that she needed to escape from the way she and Bob were together. They would get into these tiffs where she would at first feel hurt, then angry, and later withdrawn. Somewhere in the midst of these tiffs, she experienced Bob as withdrawn, and they would settle into a cold war that might last weeks. It was the terrible feeling of this kind of bonding pattern that she wanted to escape, only this part inside that drove her to escape these chronic bonding patterns with her husband was not quite conscious. This subpersonality that desired escape drove her but was not visible to her.

"The husband, Bob I'll call him, sometimes found himself dominated by thoughts of killing his wife's lover and sometimes considered having an affair himself with a woman he had met at a convention in New York. Both daydreams frightened him, particularly the murder fantasy, because in his work as a CPA he was known as a gentle, dependable, and cultured man. His fantasies of murder and of starting an affair brought on intense self-recriminations.

"The affair itself ended before they came to me, but Betty was depressed and drinking 'more than usual,' and Bob had panic attacks at his office and fought with his teenage children when he was at home.

"Their stated goals in therapy were to get rid of these terrible feelings so they could get back to feeling normal again, although they both had serious doubts about whether this could be accomplished. They had absolutely no knowledge that roaming around inside of them were many inner selves that would sometimes grab the wheel of their life and drive it into a ditch. Mostly because of this drought of awareness of their many inner selves, their marriage was fast sinking."

A MYTH OF MANY INNER SELVES

When I completed my account, Marc and I sat in silence, listening to the Stellar's blue jays, larger than the ones I was accustomed to in Texas but just as lively and bold in their ways. I had just begun my analysis of some of the subpersonalities inside Bob and Betty, but I sensed Marc had something he wanted to say before I continued.

"For some reason your client's situation reminds me of an old story, a myth you might say." Marc shifted his weight to get comfortable so he could tell me his story, and I offered my rapt attention because I knew from our previous outings that stories of his people often were unconscious associations that provided profound maps of the inner and interpersonal topography traversed by my clients and me.

His story began.

"A young woman and her five brothers went on a long journey. One day, they came to a creek which flowed through a deep and shadowy canyon, an ominous place that made them feel uneasy, though they did not know exactly why.

"They had walked a long distance and experienced stabbing hunger, so the brothers went out to hunt, each choosing his own path. When night fell, only four came back. They did not know what happened to the one who did not return. Four went out the next day, since their luck had not been good on the previous effort, but, once again, one did not return. This process repeated until all the brothers turned up lost, and so the young woman wandered alone, confused, and directionless.

"She had no food, and didn't even know how to pray to the Higher Source, because this happened thousands of years before human beings knew anything about prayer or *Wakan Tanka,* the Sacred Mystery. Starving and full of despair, she reached her rope's end, wishing she could die. A rock, not much bigger than the end of her thumb, caught her eye; indeed, it called out to her in a voice she couldn't quite understand. Yet the way seemed clear that she was to eat the rock, or at least swallow it, which she did, gulping to get it down.

"As soon as she swallowed the rock, she felt at peace, no longer suicidal. She drank what was left of her water, and at once the stone began to move within her. She felt not only happy but also strange stirrings in her belly that eventually she knew as pregnancy. In four days she gave birth to a boy, an unusual gestation period, to be sure.

"This stone boy, Inyan Hoksi was his name in the Lakota language, grew fast; indeed, in one week he grew as much as a year, maybe more. This phenomenal growth continued until he was old enough for his mother to tell him about his five uncles who had not returned. He trained for his search for his uncles through hunting small game. Soon, he embarked on a journey down into the dark canyons, promising his mother that one day he would return.

"On the first evening of his journey he smelled smoke, which he followed until he came to a tipi before which sat an old, ugly woman. Next to her, propped against the tipi walls, stood five large bundles. First she fed him, and then told him of her terrible backache. Inyan was much impressed with both her cooking and her kindly attitude toward him, although something bothered him about her. After a while, showing much pain, she implored him to walk on her back to make her feel better, a puzzling request for cure.

"Inyan Hoksi walked up and down on the old woman's back until he felt something sharp sticking out of her backbone, like a spear. Intuitively he recognized this spear, not only as a danger to him, but also the means by which she had speared his uncles. Without hesitating, he jumped high in the air and came down hard on the old woman, breaking her neck and killing her. He next built a large fire, threw the old witch in it, and burned her to ashes.

"Sitting down to rest for a moment, he heard voices coming from nearby rocks; they spoke a language he readily understood, because he was a relative of the rock people. They told him to build a little lodge of willow sticks and hides and put the five bundles he had seen near the tipi walls inside the lodge, to put red-hot stones from the fire in the middle of the lodge, and to take water in an animal skin bag to pour over the hot rocks.

"He thanked the rocks, covered the lodge with animal skins so no air could escape, and sat down, feeling the sweat rolling down his quickly heating body. The more he sweated, the more he could hear voices coming from inside the five bundles.

"On the fourth time he poured water over the rocks, he heard muffled voices coming from the sacks and saw the tight rawhide knots loosening until at last his uncles came bounding out of the bundles, breaking loose with great energy. The six of them talked and sang together, and Inyan Hoksi shouted, 'The rocks saved me, and now they saved you. From now on this sweat lodge will be sacred to us. It will give us good health and will purify us.'

"Then the uncles, along with Inyan Hoksi, journeyed back to the lip of the canyon to reunite with their mother and sister and eventually return to their tribe, bringing with them their important discovery from the depths of the canyons."

THE REALITY OF SUBPERSONALITIES

Both the beginning struggle of Bob and Betty, and the myth of Inyan Hoksi, provide a launching for this book. At this point Bob and Betty don't think of themselves as being on the transformational pathway. They are hurting and just want to get back to normal. Soon, the pain will subside somewhat, and they will be faced with whether they want a Band-Aid or something more basic—unfolding transformation.

The first task Bob and Betty have is to discover that the way they have viewed themselves is not adequate for this stage of their lives. Previously, they, like most of us, have assumed that they are a single, unified person. From their account I notice immediately that numerous aspects roam around in the illusory flow of energy that we so conveniently call *the person.*

These aspects are flows of energy that often have a reality all their own, to the point that they exist as subpersonalities within the person. What Bob and Betty notice, at first with trepidation and then with excitement, is that they are an astounding variety of parts: Betty has within her a wife, mother, a sexy twenty-two-year-old, a harsh and overbearing judge, and a remorseful child, to name a few. Bob's intense pain arises from a hurt little boy, a jealous tyrant, a self-righteous savior, and a merciless killer, all of whom were mostly unknown to him until the fateful night of the party.

Marc's association of the Stone Boy myth with Bob's and Betty's drama tastes of wisdom because the myth discloses *the notion of the many selves.* The characters of the myth speak of the many inner parts: the young-woman/mother, the five brothers, the stone boy, the witch, the rocks, the deep canyon, the sweat lodge, and the tribe. All these characters are symbols of parts of ourselves that are archetypes. How they are basic to Bob and Betty—and maybe to the reader—will unfold.

Since Betty saw herself as "one" person, she could not separate out that only a few parts of her wanted out of the marriage. Other parts were still in love with Bob, but they were now in the background, blocked out by the passionate parts. She thought she was going "crazy" because one minute her lustful self would dominate the stage of her inner consciousness and another minute the responsible mother would take over.

There are in each of us a diversity of these semiautonomous subpersonalities in various states of awareness that pull on our consciousness, and the ones that pull on us the greatest are the ones with which we identify most readily. When the paradox of the One and the Many bulges into our consciousness, it can shake the foundations. That this paradox exists in the outer world is transparently clear to the casual observer, but the existential reality in the inner world can be seismic in its proportions.

As I explore the desert wilderness with my medicine friends, the landscape pulls out of me many varied aspects. These energy flows are not present with me in the city, and they want to take over as I move deeper into the wilderness. Each time I cross the invisible line I mentioned before, a subpersonality will emerge that comes from some hidden source in my brain, perhaps the reptilian stem.

As my forays into the world of the shaman increase, I discover a hunter who already knows how to move through the countryside, a warrior who has fought a thousand battles on a sandy plain on a windy continent, and eventually a medicine man who knows ways of therapy I have not dreamed of in my usual consciousness. At first, I am seduced by these new and potent subpersonalities, but then I realize that, as with all subpersonalities, they must be channeled through a process in the person called, for lack of a better term, *the aware ego.*

It will be a fundamental assumption of this book that identifying and exploring the subpersonalities (the many) will aid in the development of awareness of the ego. This aware ego, then, views the panorama of the many selves and offers a sense of *the one.*

THE NATURE OF SUBPERSONALITIES

A subpersonality consists of an energetic organization of habit patterns, traits, complexes, and other psychological elements the center of which is an inner drive, or urge, that strives to be expressed (Assagioli, 1965). These subunits within the person can function more or less independently, can be co-operative in the interest of the whole person, or can align with other segments of the person to mount a rebellion against the whole.

The state of Texas offers an analogy. Before 1845, it functioned as an independent republic, mostly because the United States was not yet prepared to assimilate it as a state; Texas was too wild and unruly and would have made the United States too vulnerable, according to my high school history teacher. Later, it was welcomed into the union; it continued to exist in name and content but gave up its identity as a republic and existed as a subentity within a federal government. Still later, it aligned with other states in a major rebellion, and then it had to pass through a period of assimilation again.

The inner states within the federalism of the person function roughly in this order. They, like Texas or New York or Delaware, are subunits that have boundaries, enter into arguments, and often have different cultures from the whole. In some instances they speak entirely different languages. In "normal" people these boundaries are more or less permeable; the parts work with or against each other but acknowledge, sometimes grudgingly, the executive branch of the federalism. In other instances, as with multiple personality disorders, the subunits develop rigid boundaries, so that there is little communication between the inner states (Watkins & Watkins, 1981). In people who adapt in this energetic configuration, the central government has no control over the states.

When clients first begin to experience the reality of the many selves, they will make comments like Bob and Betty, where they wonder, "Am I crazy like the book about what's her name, Sybil?" They are typical in that they harbor the mistaken notion that only "crazy" people have "split personalities." I explain that we all are a collection of parts as they relate to the whole and that diagnostic terms simply describe the varying intensity and adaptations of the organism.

These subpersonalities tend to appear in pairs that are generally not in balance with each other. One tends to dominate the other; however, there is something in the energy of the subpersonalities that tends toward balance and therefore is not "happy" until it is in balance with its opposite and in harmony with the larger organism.

When I first talked to the part of Betty that wanted her to be involved in the affair, I asked the segment if she realized how much difficulty Betty was in because of the affair. That part spoke angrily. "What are you trying to do, scramble me up into scrambled eggs with all those other whimps inside her? I won't have it. That is why I got her attention in the first place; I wanted to get her out of this scrambled eggs thing with her husband and kids. I was just scrambled in with the rest of them, and I don't like it. I want to have my own say-so. If you are going to promote more of that, I just won't show up at these meetings she brings me to."

THE BABBLE OF PARTS

"If we are a tangle of many parts, how on earth can we possibly know what to do with them. I will be in the middle of a complicated accounting problem, and this jealous rage will overwhelm me: It will just come in and totally crowd out my usual way of thinking and torment me."

Bob speaks well for an experience most of us have to one degree or another, if not with a jealous subpart then with some other unit of bothersome energy.

"Then, I can't work. I am obsessed with fantasies about how to get revenge. Since the beginning of our therapy, I now can recognize this energy when it comes on me, but what on earth do I do with it? And when I say that I recognize it, it is only in the middle of the experience that I realize for several hours I have been captured by this energy. Or maybe, days later, I will recognize that I have been a total bastard toward Betty and my kids because this jealous-revengeful guy has completely taken over the driver's seat of my car."

Herein resides the block to Bob's evolution of self: to develop in life, he has overidentified with certain parts of himself—such as the part of himself that follows rules, the part that expects perfection, and the part that is superadequate. These parts mentioned above—the hurt little boy, the jealous avenger, and the bastard—have been pushed into the depths of his unconscious (the dark and shadowy canyon of the myth of Inyan Hoksi), as personae non gratae. These parts have been tied up in bundles, as the myth suggests, and we can only hear their muffled voices under certain conditions.

Because he has given them little attention, they have become more and more sour. When they do gain a moment on the stage of Bob's life, they act like the witches in the story. So the journey of the transforming selves begins with the recognition of the many selves. Some of them are overworked (overidentified aspects); some of them are pushed to the edges of consciousness (disowned selves); some have never reached consciousness at all (unknown selves.)

THE SANITY OF HEARING VOICES

Now surfaces a curious paradox: A popular notion has it, as I indicated above, that hearing voices means a person is crazy. A common comment goes like this: "Well, I may talk to myself, but I'm not really crazy unless I start answering."

To the contrary, I suggest that we all hear voices, and that the way to evolve is to hear them better, not to stop them. Hearing them better means listening with ever expanding awareness that then becomes available to the part of us that is a choice maker. Craziness is not having the equipment to listen to ourselves; evolving sanity is having the equipment, plus the courage. Sanity expands as we learn to facilitate the speaking of the voices, the listening, and the replying through an aware ego.

In this vein, when I was twelve years old, a teacher introduced me to the notion of seeking out a vision and listening to voices. In a conversation after class, she told me of the Kwehar-rehnuh Komatsi custom of the young male seeking out *puha,* the Komatsi word for medicine power. Perhaps she talked to me of such matters because she had known my grandfather, who had come to the High Plains of Texas, known as the *Llano Estacado,* on horseback. Whatever the reason, we made an energetic connection that would influence me greatly.

She pointed me in the direction of exploring the purpose of such a vision quest through a term paper. I eventually found that the goal of a quest was to hear the voice of an animal spirit that would be a guide throughout a person's life by connecting with some inner voice within the vision seeker.

As a public school teacher, she had little interest in the vision quest itself. Her interest was in awakening my curiosity through pointing me in the direction of this subject and through putting material in my hands that spoke of such matters. As I searched, mouth ajar, the sources explained that sometimes the animal spirit appeared in the form of an actual animal like a wolf or an eagle. Sometimes, however, the animal appeared only in the mind of the seeker who could see and hear its instructions at crucial times throughout life.

These statements tickled my pubescent innards.

When I wondered to myself if the animals existed as we know them, the sources explained that it didn't make any difference to the Kwehar-renuh (Antelope People), who did not differentiate between these two levels of reality. My twelve-year-old imagination had been fired. The myths that I had discovered explained to me that the voices and visions I heard and saw did not make me crazy, something I had considered a probability.

Could there be room for both the eagle and the owl? I wondered and saw the possibilities.

In retrospect I can see that I latched onto these myths as a way to help me interpret the many inner selves that were appearing on the inner stage of my life at that time. According to the Komatsi myths, they were to be valued.

The Komatsi not only listened to these voices and sought visions, they also acted out a variety of voices. They had people in the tribe who painted themselves black and white and did everything backwards, including riding their horses. Some would do this for a period of time, while others would perform these backwards acts most of their lives.

They were called *contraries.* They were greatly valued by the tribe as acting out energy flows that kept the community flexible and alert.

Early anthropologists noticed that shamans listened to many voices and encouraged activities like that of the contraries, and they mistakenly interpreted this behavior as being psychotic. They taught that the shamans were borderline psychotics who were only tolerated by the tribes. More recent anthropological studies have revealed that shamans are the most stable, intelligent, and, often, productive people in their tribes.

In tribal ways those who remained content with hearing only their everyday voices were viewed as less powerful and less aware of themselves and their context. Under certain conditions one would receive an especially elaborate vision, and that person would be described by the Kwewar-renuh as a *puhakut,* a shaman or medicine person. In other words, the more visions one saw and voices one heard, the more *puha (power that comes from increased awareness)* one had. This point of view stands in sharp contrast to our culture's.

The more I have crossed the line into the ways of the *puhakut,* the more I realize that this pathway that was closely aligned with Nature encouraged people to dive deep into currents of energy within realms that looked "crazy" to the outside world. The function of the *puhakut* was to guide the seeker as he went into a vision and voice of a subpersonality that was connected with an animal spirit.

Could it be that the way through what we call abnormal behavior and psychopathology is to journey deeper into the turbulent vortexes of energy? Could it be that, by medicating and silencing the voices, we are blocking the seeker from going through the energy? But only by such energizing can the ego have the awareness it needs to make informed decisions about what to do with a particular subpersonality.

From time to time a contemporary psychotherapist such as R.D. Laing (1964) will suggest this pathway. However, it is not often recognized that the experience to navigate such treacherous inner terrain lies backwards in the mists of prehistory where the ancient shamans would lead people on such a journey. In their culture they had the support of the tribe, as did the seekers. There was no vision or voice too bizarre to be heard. Each voice had its place, and most of them would take many moons to interpret. They were not concerned, because they had much time and because the landscape in which they lived would help the person through the sometimes frightening energies. Through their quests and sweat lodges, the tribes allowed them to journey into the heart of the subpersonality to hear what it had to say.

Then, the voice had to be spoken before the tribal council with the interpretation of the *puhakut,* resulting in the council of voices. The reason that a person does crazy behavior in our society, I believe, is that they do not have an aware ego to listen to the voices and to interpret the visions. They are victims of whatever energy enters the stage of their inner life to dominate them, and they do not have a guide who has been willing to enter his voices and visions.

If the guides do not know their own "crazy" subpersonality, they will be frightened by the voices heard by the seeker. I encourage seekers to explore the voices and visions of the many subpersonalities within only when they have the support of guides who have been willing to enter the fire of their own voices. Even having a guide is not enough to explore some inner flows of energy; one must also have a tribe, a supportive community of people who will act as an adjunct to the aware ego of the seeker.

Ultimately, we "two-legs" are lost without a tribe. We in the U.S.A. have a nation, but we have lost our tribes and are fast losing our families. A person can seek psychotherapy, but without the tribe the transformation will be limited. A person can enter all kinds of learning situations with a variety of gurus, including sweat lodges and vision quests, but without tribal support some voices will not be heard. Even if they are heard, there will be trouble for the individual if there is no tribal community to help the person through the journey.

THE INNER COUNCIL

At an early age, then, I sought these Komatsi myths to understand my developing inner family. There was one inner segment filled with rage, and he was not welcome either in my family of origin or at school. There was a merciless critic and perfectionist who demanded results at school and in athletics; these parts were valued by my culture. There was a terrified little boy who did not know if he could become a man, and no one seemed interested in listening to him. There was a spiritual adventurer who asked unusual questions of teachers, coaches, and ministers. There was an emerging lover who lusted after the young woman two blocks down the street.

Bob and Betty were each discovering their inner families in the early stages of therapy. It slowly dawned on them that some of their inner family of selves liked being married and some didn't. They traced some of these inner segments as having originated in their parents' inner lives, but so far they did not know what to do with this emerging awareness of the inner family. Soon, they pushed me to guide them toward some way of managing this inner family, especially the ones that were skeletons in the inner family's closet.

REFERENCES

Assagioli, R. (1965). *Psychosynthesis.* New York: Penguin.

Campbell, J. (1969). *The masks of god: Primitive mythology.* New York: Penguin.

Castaneda, C. (1968). *The teachings of don Juan: A yaqui way of knowledge.* New York: Ballantine.

Eliade, M. (1964). *Shamanism: Archaic techniques of ecstasy.* Princeton, NJ: Princeton University Press.

Harner, M. (1982). *The way of the shaman.* New York: Bantam.

Jung, C. (1933). *Modern man in search of a soul.* New York: Harcourt Brace.

Laing, R.D. (1964). *Politics of the family.* London: Tavistock.

Watkins, J.G., & Watkins, H.H. (1981). Ego-state therapy. In I.E. Abt & I.R. Stuarts (Eds.), *The newer therapies: A source book.* New York: Van Nostrand Rheingold.

2

The Sacred Bundle of Awareness

The young warrior, David Hawkface, settled into my rented car as we rolled through a valley in south-central Colorado that stretched between snowcapped peaks with Spanish names. No time for skiing was this warm day, yet summer tourists were still far away. After grilling me on my experience on the Pathway—a shorthand reference to the Native American approach to growth and transformation—Hawkface lapsed into a brooding silence. The dust from our wheels scared up an occasional jackrabbit.

An hour or so later he spoke, "You seem like a man I could tell my shame to. Will you listen?"

I nodded in consent, but his request was more complicated than it sounded. Lately, I had found that, when I attempted to listen, my inner voices drowned out my ears. At that very moment, his questioning of my progress in Native American ways had stirred up a variety of inner voices. One voice criticized him for what appeared to be his self-righteousness over his Native blood. Another wandered off and wanted to go play in the mountains. Another wanted to argue with Hawkface and tell him of the ancient tribal prophesy that the non-Indian would play a crucial role in the transformation of the planet by taking up native medicine ways.

All of these inner voices interfered with my listening to David.

"Last spring," Hawkface began, "I received a Sacred Pipe from an honored medicine man after I had been through years of preparation. It was given jointly to me and my mate as a family pipe."

"We were charged to use this pipe to develop our own awareness and to enrich our relationship. It was not a medicine pipe, because we were just beginners in medicine ways, but it was the most important thing that had ever happened to either of us.

"Yet we found ourselves bickering over how to use the pipe. As in the past, we fought over many other matters as well. Then one day, while we were in the midst of a fight, I stalked across the parking lot of a shopping mall carrying the pipe to my truck. Lost in the angry things I wanted to say to my mate, I wasn't paying attention to what I was doing and dropped the sacred bundle in which I had my pipe wrapped. The pipe seemed alive and actually felt like it was squirming in my arms to get my attention. It squirmed until it seemed to pop out of my arms and then bounced off the pavement.

"Terrified, I hurriedly unlaced the leather that kept the pipe secure in the bundle to see if it was damaged in any way.

"My worst fears shot through my body stabbing my heart. The red stone bowl of the pipe lay broken near the circular opening.

"Naturally, my mate blamed me, and then, after several weeks of anguish, we decided to split. After years of work, I have no pipe. I have no mate. I think I am the most unworthy person in the world."

We rode on.

The inner voices that I referred to above echoed in my head as they had the entire time he had been talking. I had, in fact, listened to very little of his tragic story. I mumbled something that therapists often say when they haven't been listening closely: "I hear your pain."

Maybe I had heard more than I thought, because I could feel the pulsations of his pain emanating from his body. Something about his tale sent a charge of energy into my body. I don't know whether it helped him to pour out his story, because I didn't see him again for years. Nearly a decade passed, and I forgot Hawkface altogether, except to hear that he had involved himself in piercing his chest and hanging from ropes, maybe to purify himself of his shame.

One night, after I had spent time on a wilderness mountain, a powerful dream came to me. The main character in the dream was a weathered Native American man by the name of O-nee-ha. He had appeared in my dreams at crucial times since, as a boy, I had seen the fight between the owl and the eagle. Without knowing why, I associated him with the cave from which I had seen the fight on that morning so many years before.

By this time O-nee-ha had become much more than a dream figure. He at first was a teacher sent from the mists of the land of archetypes, that domain of ancient energetic wisdom that is sometimes called the collective unconscious. A key figure in my inner council of voices throughout my childhood as a so-called imaginary friend, he later looked out at me through the eyes of a Native American man, known by a similar name, with whom I walked the East Texas woods as a young adult.

In this particular dream he was dressed in old buckskin pants, a leather vest with no shirt, and long braids tied off with colorful pieces of animal skin. He smelled faintly of sweat, campfire smoke in his hair, and newly cut sage.

"I come to tell you why David Hawkface was sent to you by the Powers of the Universe," he began his dreamlike communication. "He came to tell you about broken pipes and sacred bundles that are dropped because you need to know about that in yourself."

He cleared his throat and waited for the image of the broken pipe and dropped bundle to sink in, then continued, "Your pipe was given to you to help you listen to yourself and to the Sounds of the Universe, so that your awareness can increase. The pipe is at the heart of the sacred eagle bundle of awareness, and it will be broken if you do not learn better how to listen. The pipe is alive, as Hawkface learned. It will jump in front of your face to raise your awareness if it has to. Your pipe is especially to help people listen to those they love very deeply, beginning with the ones inside."

As usual, O-nee-ha hit me between the eyes with his truth, because I was having trouble listening to him in my dream at that very moment. I wanted to wake up and escape his piercing brown eyes.

Sensing my struggle, O-nee-ha tacked in a different direction. "I want to remind you of a few scenes from the myth called 'The Many Colored Buffalo.' Maybe it will help you understand.

"As you recall, a beautiful woman appeared on the plains of Turtle Island to two Lakota hunters."

I relaxed and smiled, because O-nee-ha referred to our continent in a quaint way as "Turtle Island," the description used by Natives before the Europeans arrived. He continued.

"One of them was passionate and made a pass at her. He ended up being eaten by her animal helpers, the snakes. Frightened, the other one returned to his elders to tell of this mysterious event and to relay the message that she was coming.

"She certainly had their attention with the snakes and all. Anyway, she walked into their lodge and unwrapped the sacred bundle that she had brought from the Sacred Mystery, *Wakan Tanka.* Out of the bundle she lifted the pipe. 'This pipe,' she explained to them, 'was to be used for their growth, development, and transformation.'

"To dramatize the transforming abilities of the pipe, she changed first into a small brown buffalo calf, then a large white buffalo, and finally into a huge black buffalo.

"You know this myth well, but I want you to learn something new from it today. Hawkface's pipe was broken because his relationship was broken. It was attempting to relay that truth to him. It was also broken so he could tell you about your inability to listen to him or yourself and how that lack of awareness breaks down relationships.

"This is the truth of the broken pipe in the sacred bundle: It breaks open your awareness, as it did for the ancient Lakota. It opens the way to new parts to come to you to speak. It helps you listen to them. It facilitates the council of your inner voices."

With that, O-nee-ha abruptly wiped his hands, first across his brown face and then on his buckskin pants, stood up, and walked away. Just before he disappeared in the fog that surrounds the land of archetypes and unconsciousness, he turned and crinkled his nose.

PONDERING O-NEE-HA

When I returned to a usual state of consciousness, I pondered what O-nee-ha had had to say. It is fitting that O-nee-ha first tells the myth of the Many Colored Buffalo in this book, because he has been the most enduring influence in my life, as he has joined hands with my many teachers through the years.

This first telling of the myth is brief, as O-nee-ha is prone to be. The myth graphically describes the seating of our inner council of selves, the pain and travail we find ourselves in, and the coming of an energy that will open our awareness, symbolized and actualized by the pipe. O-nee-ha recognizes the struggle we humans have when we are deluged with many inner voices that contend for our attention. He attempts to offer a way to listen to these many voices through the awareness brought in the sacred bundle.

THE DEVELOPMENT OF THE INNER COUNCIL OF SELVES

Not long after my experience with David Hawkface, Bob brought up the issue of the babble of inner voices and the difficulty of listening to them because more than one would speak at a time. "Maybe it would help," he suggested, "if I had some idea of how these many parts came into being inside."

In the back of my mind, I could hear the words of O-nee-ha speaking of the importance of awareness. In the front of my mind, I asked Bob if he would like to see a movie of the development of his inner selves.

I further explained to him that this movie would be in his mind and in mine (and now in yours).

He nodded, "Yes."

I asked him if he could imagine that he came down his mother's birth canal and plopped into the atmosphere of this planet as a pure being, a unit of energy that was ready to soak up information about living in relationship. At that moment his psychic, physical, and spiritual fingerprint was present in the form of a tiny baby.

Could he, I further asked, imagine on his inner movie screen the look on the baby's face?

Again, he nodded affirmatively.

Then, I asked him to take over the movie, as I do you, in order to imagine how he developed.

At first he was silent, and then I added, "See if you can imagine a scene where you are learning how to survive in your world."

"I can see myself as a little baby just learning to walk. I explore near a coffee table. I touch something, and it pokes me with a sharp edge. I recoil, crying."

Then I asked him if something else, another energy, showed up to help him with his situation.

"Yes, a force inside seems to hold back my hand the next time I have an impulse to touch the sharp object, scissors I think they are."

This development of the protector energy was natural and necessary for Bob and all of us, because something is needed to stand between the unit of pure being in him as a child and the dangers of the world.

I invited Bob to continue with creating his inner movie.

"The next thing I know, I have rules about everything in my life. Rules about not playing in my poop, rules about not throwing food, rules about not going across the street, rules about not peeing in the yard. This new protector part is a genius about picking up what the big people in my world wanted and didn't want and translating them into rules so I could survive."

"Then what happens?" I ask.

"I guess I am about four now, and I feel this tremendous anger to lash out at so many rules. There is this part that hates to be confined by the rules. He argues with the protector. The two of them start a fight. It's bloody."

I encourage him to continue, though it is now painful.

"About this same time, I feel critical. I criticize myself for all kinds of things. Somehow it seems better to criticize myself before my Mommie can get to me when she yells at me about stuff I do that I know I shouldn't.

"The part of me that wants to please my Mommie and Daddy gets bigger, but not any bigger than the anger. The guy that makes the rules pushes the anger down into a prison cell and promotes the one that wants to please my folks. The guy in jail yells and yells; it seems there are others in there with him."

Bob's face contorts, and I ask him if the movie continues.

"This is all I can do today."

Bob didn't arrive at the point for him to start to school in the movie, the time when the rules would require him to wear shoes, not to look out the window, and not to introduce his imaginary playmates to the class. He didn't get to the part of his inner movie where he repressed his capacity for talking to animals, climbing trees, and playing in the dirt.

His inner movie was cut short, but the drift was clear to him and to me. Many parts developed to help him survive, and they began to dominate his inner stage and thus blocked his awareness. They now overlaid the fingerprint of pure being and shoved the more natural parts into the background, along with others that proved unacceptable to his immediate environment.

WORD FROM PRISON

Shortly after the above experience, Bob had a dream. In the dream he was going on a trip to an island off the coast of Washington. His car broke down on the way, and he became aware of a building beside the road. On closer look, he could see it was a prison. The prisoners climbed over the wall and came toward him, making threatening gestures as they came. He woke up in a sweat.

Bob's selves that had been thrown into prison by his protectors now poured over the wall; they revolted against this arrangement, just as his wife's sexual rebel had. They wanted him to listen, but at this time in Bob's life there was little awareness available for the listening process, so he avoided them as best he could. They would continue to appear in his dreams, as we shall see in later chapters.

THE BODY SPEAKS

These inner prisoners not only speak through dreams; they also enlist the body to speak on their behalf. When we do not have a listening process, they step up the intensity of their messages through the body, usually through a pain. Like the broken pipe, they clamor for anyone to hear them.

One morning in my mid-twenties, I first noticed that my body was attempting to speak to me. Out of town on a trip to conduct seminars, I looked into the mirror as I dressed. There I saw angry red welts across my shoulder, especially my right shoulder. Immediately, the inner critic lit into the welts, telling them to go away; they were an inconvenience. This kind of listening did not help; they just got worse.

Miserable, I sought medical help, but nothing would make the welts disappear. At my wit's end, I sought out psychotherapy. With the help of a therapist, I developed enough awareness to begin listening to the welts. First, I had to quiet down the inner critic who didn't like the welts. It turned out that the welts spoke on behalf of some hidden parts that had been thrown into prison. They popped out on the page as I wrote in my journal:

"We are here because you don't like your work."

"What do you mean?" I protested. "I have a Master's degree in the field. I am doing well."

"You guys who are currently in the driver's seat may like the work Taegel does, but we, the welts, represent some other parts that don't. The place where you work is so rigid that we can't express ourselves. Besides, look at yourself. You have no color. That's another reason why we are here: to remind you how boring you have become."

Soon, I applied for a doctoral program that would allow me to enhance my skills in psychotherapy and begin a practice outside the institutional context where I was at the time. The day I received my acceptance, the welts disappeared. In a few months, however, they returned. "Look!" I wrote in my journal, "I did what you asked. Why are you back?"

"Did you think you would get off that easy?" They seemed to pulsate in the mirror. "We now have to speak to you about the family that you grew up in and your marriage. You have problems you won't face. These guys that run your life tell you that everything is just fine. Well, it isn't."

THE SURVIVAL SELVES CANNOT LISTEN

Messages like these from dreams and the body bring the transformation process to a crucial point. The *survival* or *primary selves*—the protector/controller, the critic, the pusher, the pleaser, and others—recognize something fundamental is wrong with the organism. The very strategies that they devised as part of the solution are now at the forefront of the problem. The more they try to control things through their heavy-handed tactics, the more the hidden selves revolt.

The more the hidden selves revolt, the more the primary selves have to work with the alarm clock of anxiety, then the alarm itself gets out of control in a feedback loop that is the source of anxiety attacks. This anxiety then joins hands with the survival selves on the inner stage; they attempt to listen to the hidden selves.

They cannot.

This kind of listening is futile.

These selves are not made to listen; they are for survival. They are what dominated me when I attempted to listen to Hawkface, while his survival selves blocked out his awareness as the pipe jumped in his arms.

To use another analogy, the hidden selves are in the inner womb of the person attempting to come down the birth canal. Unless they have an adequate energy to receive them in the birthing room, they will get stuck in the birth canal and poison the system.

THE SACRED BUNDLE PROVIDES A CUSHION

Needed in the birthing room is a listening presence that can "hear" the hidden selves as they come through. Aware listening provides the cushion necessary for safety as they come into consciousness. Only when awareness is added to the ego space can the kind of listening necessary be provided. If we leave the birthing to our usual selves that operate without much awareness, the vulnerable selves will be further injured.

In the myth of the Many Colored Buffalo, awareness is symbolized by the bundle brought to the tribal setting. In the myth the space where the tribe sits is called the *lodge,* symbolic of our own ego space. Thus, the myth tells us we need the awareness brought by the bundle and the pipe to aid in this birth.

THE AWARE EGO APPEARS

When we add awareness to our ego space, then we have an ego that is aware of both the survival selves and the selves coming down the birth canal. *This aware ego can listen adequately to both classes of selves. The awareness that has been added to the ego allows a process of alert choice making.* It is important to remember throughout this book that, when I used the phrase *aware ego,* I refer to this process, not a thing.

Return for a moment to Bob's escaping prisoners. Bob needs to talk to Betty about his rage concerning the affair, but he is afraid to, because

Betty is so quick with words that sting him. I ask him if there is any energy inside that can protect him while he talks to Betty.

He looks totally blank. He has absolutely no awareness of any part that can help, because his ego space is so dominated by an energy that wants to please Betty. I invite him to look at the prisoners as they pour over the wall. Reluctantly, he agrees.

"Do you see any animals?" I ask him.

A surprised look bounces across his face. "Yes, I do. I see a bear."

I then ask those selves who sit in his ego space, the survival selves, if I can talk to Bob's bear. They agree. His bear tells me he is eight feet tall, weighs over a thousand pounds, and can protect Bob from anyone. He explains that he doesn't even need to growl at Betty. All he needs to do is stand behind Bob in case Bob needs him. Even so, I invite the bear inside Bob to offer a small growl just to let us know what he is like. To Bob's surprise and delight (as well as mine), the inner bear lets out a growl that shakes the office.

After listening to Bob's bear, I summarize for him what the bear has said while he stands in another part of the room. He soaks up this information from the aware state that is neutral to both the primary selves and the hidden selves. He then returns to his ego space to sit down. As he returns, he brings with him a new awareness of one of his new selves. The bear has landed on the cushion of his new awareness. Had the awareness not been there, the bear might have landed hard and been in a bad mood. It is not a good idea to get a bear in a nasty mood.

Now Bob had the choice of paying attention to his anxiety about speaking to Betty or of bringing in his bear. This example describes a process called the *awakening of an aware ego.* Here are the elements in the awakening process: the ego space is dominated by a cluster of survival selves. After they trust the therapist, they give permission for him or her to listen to one of the hidden selves.

The hidden self speaks at length. In this way the client fully enters and experiences the subunit of energy that is the hidden self. He or she then emerges to listen to a summary. As he or she listens from a neutral spot, awareness dawns. He or she then carries that awareness back to the ego space. For the moment the seeker enjoys a process that I, and others, call the aware ego.

THE AWARE EGO AND THE MIDWIFE

Continuing with the birth analogy, it is the job of the facilitator (psychotherapist, shaman, or otherwise) to provide an expressive context whereby the aware ego can develop. In the beginning of the transformation process, the aware ego and the midwife (facilitator) join hands to receive a variety of hidden selves as they come through into the consciousness of the seeker. Later, the aware ego often facilitates itself.

In either case the transformational spiral will inevitably lead to a point where inner animals and other primitive energies like Bob's bear will appear in the birth canal, calling out to be pulled through. These primitive creatures usually appear after the seeker has been on the transformational pathway for some period of time and after the therapist has acted as midwife for a number of hidden subpersonalities that are less primitive and prefer the safety of an office or workshop setting.

Eventually, though, a few of these inner animals will peek their heads out in the therapist's office, as happened with Bob, but this peeking out is just to test the waters and see if the midwife has enough awareness to know what to do next. In order for them to be fully birthed, the midwife will have to move the process outdoors.

A certain quality of awareness in the seeker comes forth outside that does not come forth indoors. Plus, these inner voices, like the bear, closely associate themselves with Nature, and the ego must be firmly linked with Nature in order for the class of awareness needed for their birth to be present. These inner voices won't fully speak unless they feel fresh air on the face of the organism and unless they hear the sound of wild things around them.

The midwife who births this class of energy in the seeker must be fully acclimated to the wilds. The shaman is the one who knows about rocks, trees, mountains, animals, fire, and water—the world outside the four walls. He or she has learned how to co-operate with these living creatures in the providing of listening awareness as a cushion for the primitive subpersonality as it comes through into consciousness.

In short, it is the inner shaman, as the myth makes clear, who can be the ears and eyes of the aware ego to perceive the inner subpersonalities that seek attention from the subterranean strata of the personality. If the client/seeker senses the psychotherapist has a shaman inside or access to a shaman, then these energies will vibrate. When this happens, incredible possibilities for transformation open.

Marv was a brilliant psychologist who worked with a large institution. He mainly had the responsibility of research in that job and came for supervision and training because his original dream of being a psychotherapist somehow got sidetracked. He made rapid progress in developing clinical skills. His caseload includes one client in particular who moved well along the spiral pathway of transformation.

To his delight Marv accessed awareness in himself and facilitated awareness in his client, Rick we'll call him, about a number of primary and then hidden subpersonalities. Rick progressed to the point where he added bundle after bundle of awareness to his ego space, so that he made better and better choices for himself. Together, seeker and therapist joined hands in awareness to midwife these subunits of energy as they slid down the birth canal into Rick's ego space.

Then the process bogged down. Marv found his mind wandering. Rick missed appointments and balked at diving into the subpersonalities to experience them. He preferred to talk from his rational energy about them. Marv brought this situation to our supervision session. Rick had grown up in an alcoholic family where his father, just returned from military service, abused the children physically. Week after week Marv had enabled Rick to bring these wounded little inner children through to the surface of consciousness, but now the process screeched to a halt.

Something was missing.

Finally, I asked Marv to bring an audio tape in from the interview where he first heard of Rick's physical abuse. In it Rick told about how his father beat him severely with an oak branch because Rick had spilled a soft drink on the seat of the car. Rick explained that all the time he was being beaten, he was almost glad because his daily beating would then be over, and he could leave the family setting and go to his special place.

On the audio I clearly heard a major voice shift when Rick spoke of the special place. My ears perked up. I asked Marv to stop the recorder and invited the team of supervisees to guess what his special place would be. Some guessed a closet, others a club house, and others projected an attic.

I turned the recorder back on: Rick went on to mention a special place in the woods.

As I heard these words, I became excited. At first Marv did not know why I was so hopeful. It was my inner shaman who recognized that some basic and natural part of Rick was attempting to come through. I explained to Marv how there were some inner parts that needed the mid-wife to join hands with the outdoors so that awareness could be deepened. The supervision group then suggested that Marv take a brief walk with his client, sit under a tree, and invite him to describe the special place from his childhood.

Marv followed this lead. To his immense surprise, Rick poured out an energy that related to the woods behind his house. He described a lovely meadow that had a soft moss floor, divided in the middle by a gentle creek. To this place Rick would take his beloved dog and, as he lay with his back on the ground, looking at the clouds, lick his wounds.

This meadow was an inner subunit of energy, repressed from childhood but still living deep in the caverns of Rick's soul, just waiting to come through into his consciousness to aid in the transforming process. It could not come through until Marv added some awareness to his own ego space as the midwife.

Marv did not yet know that there were many animals in the meadow that were also available to help him in the therapy process. He did not yet know that there were animals near where he and Rick sat under the tree that wanted to help. He did not know that the Sacred Mystery had many sacred bundles of awareness available to him as the midwife, both inside him and his client and outside. He did not know that the sacred bundle that carried the pipe would lead to a buffalo that could change colors, transforming before the eyes of the council of voices.

He would learn about that later. It was not yet time for him to explore that part of himself, the shaman, who could be the "ears" to listen for hidden animal energies within and without. For the time being, those of us supervising him could invite him to teach his client how to use the image of the meadow as a healing balm when the pain of the memories became severe.

There would be a day when Marv could facilitate Rick in calling on the dusky smell of the moist leaves in the meadow. There would be a time when the two of them would learn how to wrap the energy of the leaves, the warmth of the sun, and the music of the creek around the bruises and cuts on his wounded, inner child.

Little did Marv know that he was near the boundary that lies between the psychotherapist and the shaman. He thought he had just been introduced to another intervention of psychotherapy, and he had. As a psychotherapist, he was learning how to participate in the pulling through of Rick's wounded selves, those injured in the abuse. These wounded selves appreciated the safety of Marv's indoor office.

But it was much more.

He was learning how to be a midwife who could carry a sacred pipe of awareness, an awareness that could pull through primitive energies that would respond only to the listening of a person fully connected to Nature. He was laying the groundwork for finding his own animal helpers. Until he did, his client Rick would have to wait.

"OK! OK!" Bob and Betty might say if they were reading this book, "we have your point about needing awareness in the ego space, but this whole thing is taking a long time, and we want to get on with it. You therapists never go fast enough. Plus, we have no interest whatsoever in the out-of-doors. Our idea of roughing it is the Hyatt Regency, so get on with making our marriage better."

3

THE HUNTER SELVES

Meanwhile, back at the mesa, my Creek Indian friend, Marc, and I continue a conversation that pertains to Bob's and Betty's beginning the transforming process, especially their rush to "solve their problems."

"This obsession with hurrying up is a principal difference between the healing of our medicine ways, the way of the *Ahe-Cha-Chay,* and what I observe of you psychotherapists." Marc is picking up on a subject we often discuss—the different domains of the shaman and the psychotherapist.

"When you get back to Houston, I want you to try something that may affect your work. Search out a tree not too far from your office and sit down with it in any way that you like. Stay with the tree in physical contact for a few minutes each working day and see what happens. Try this experiment until you notice something important in yourself. There is an actual spirit in the tree. You seem to prefer the word *energy* to *spirit,* but whatever you call it, see if you can make contact. This is something we do in my tribe to train hunters, and a medicine man uses this energy from the hunter as a foundation for all healing."

By providing me with this assignment, Marc offered me another entrance into the rich secrets of the shaman, but these assignments, which I have received from different sources over a long period of time, require persistent experimentation, not to mention discipline. An incredible web of power lies at the base of the work of the shaman, but this power is not accessible without the discipline of frequent contact with the unconscious and its connection to the Interconnective Energy of the Universe, *Wakan Tanka.*

This common ground between psychotherapy and the medicine ways of various Native American tribes can be explored by those who are willing to launch into new inner territory, and usually my experiments in this direction result in fresh awarenesses about various subpersonalities of the inner lodge.

Still, as I contemplate his suggestion, I encounter reservations. The part of me that concerns itself with what other people think shows up and speaks. "If anyone sees you trying to learn from a tree, they will think you have one wheel off in the sand."

AN ENCOUNTER WITH A TREE

Before long, though, I notice a magnolia tree near the parking lot of my office, and one morning near sunrise I begin the experiment. I choose that hour to avoid people who might think a few pages are missing out of my book. At first, I feel the bark; then I put my arms around the trunk and hold on. To my surprise, an energy of sorts flows into me, a strength to face the day.

After just a few moments, I become self-conscious and let go. The intimacy of this encounter shocks me, and I am not sure how to digest this feeling of closeness with a living creature that is not a mammal. Something from my childhood stirs within as I recall days spent under the arms of an old pear tree with whom I had an intimate relationship throughout my youth. A friend of mine who is a nutritional expert has been talking to me about not eating mammals because their link is so close to humans. He argues not to eat anything that has a brain, but I can't imagine at this moment that any creature, including other humans, can be more conscious than this tree.

The roots of the tree pattern themselves on the ground so that I fit nicely there, while the trunk supports my back. I sit, and the desire to push ahead leaves me. I notice ants crawling on the ground, the ornate designs of fallen leaves, a spider web, and other living creatures. As the months pass by, the smells of the tree change as the magnolia blossoms come and go; they spin off a lemon odor I never noticed before.

The behavior of the squirrels comes to my attention, and I mention it to a artist I know who has a sharp eye for observation. He invites me to observe the squirrels to see if I can figure out what they do with their feces. Week after week at the base of the tree I observe them, and I never see any of their droppings. Rats, mice, roaches, deer, cats, and dogs all leave their calling cards. Why not squirrels? Closer observation must be required to penetrate this puzzle, but I will leave that to other naturalists. Still, the process of observing seems fundamentally important in a way that I cannot at first put my hand on.

I attempt to explain this experiment to a colleague and how it relates to transformation of selves, and with a not-so-straight face he asks, "Do you call this tree therapy or are you just squirrely?"

THE EYE OF THE OBSERVER

His comments notwithstanding, there is a connection. Maybe not directly, but an aspect of me speaks at the inner tribe of selves that has long been disowned: the observer self, one of the hunter selves that notices very carefully the natural world that surrounds human beings. What I observe in the beginning is not as important as the attitude of observing.

The initial stage of the transforming process begins with this awakening ability to observe the inner world with increasing detachment. In the earlier stages of growth in therapy, moments of observation come primarily through the therapist. As the process unfolds, the seeker/client will increasingly observe himself. Both the therapist and the shaman can look for this observer self to develop in the client. Until this observing energy transfers from the therapist to the client, the process is stuck in the initial phase.

Marv is, as I mentioned, a brilliant psychologist in his early thirties who comes to supervision because he is unhappy with his research-oriented position in a large institution. He is trapped by a sizable salary and something else he cannot put his hand on. He is likeable but has few friends and feels especially alienated from men. He is successful but works obsessively, without emotional or spiritual reward.

He would like to relax more, but he spends his spare time volunteering at a low-income clinic or attending workshops. When he slows down, he notices a buzzing type of energy that will not let him relax. He reports this inner "fizz" to his supervision group, and the group invites him to extend an attitude of observing to a Thanksgiving dinner he plans to spend with his family of origin. To his great surprise he discovers through this observing energy that his father too has a subpersonality that will not allow him to relax.

Marv, through these observations, has taken the first steps in realizing that there is a self that is out of control, that this self has had free reign in pushing and pulling him in first one direction and then another, and that he has withdrawal symptoms if he attempts to disengage from this "fizz" type of energy. Just as caffeine provides an upper for his system, so this compulsion to work drives him and provides a daily upper. When this energy swerves out of control, Marv describes the experience as similar to that of an alcoholic who takes another hit off the bottle.

It is a terrifying fact of human existence that we humans do not generally run our lives from an aware position: the functioning ego is generally clouded over by these subpersonalities. What's even more scary is that we often don't observe any of this process unless we allow that aspect to come forth in our personalities. We become so identified with these subflows of energy that the ego cannot call on an observing aspect. We immerse ourselves in the forest so thoroughly that we cannot see the trees.

Bob's intense jealousy still rushes on the scene each time he cannot account for Betty's whereabouts, but now in the midst of the jealous rage a tiny part of him observes. He cannot yet manage this jealousy, because he doesn't know enough about it to manage it. He does not yet have the attitude of the observer, a mental framework similar to that of a detective at a scene of a crime.

Still, he catches a brief glimpse of it and how powerfully it dominates him. What he sees terrifies him. This flow of jealous energy is so powerful that it wants to dominate his every thought and behavior. It will not let go of him, no matter how he tries. He will gain just a moment's distance from the jealousy and resolve that he will not say anything else to Betty about her affair. Then the jealousy will overtake him, and he will spout out a series of accusations that totally befuddle him, just because he cannot account for a few minutes of her time.

He has been in therapy for several months, and his jealousy is just as intense. The main difference now is that he can observe it. While he is in the midst of a jealous tirade, he hears a fledgling voice: "Look at what you are doing, Bob."

He now can record in his journal his observations about these outbursts, but he still does not know enough about the jealous part of him to be able to manage it and keep that energy from disrupting his marriage. He hates the jealousy so much that he cannot look at it very long. He makes only a few observations, and then he blanks it out of his mind.

When he returns to therapy the next week, he is overjoyed at the power of his observations. All he has to do, it seems, is to observe closely one of the undesirable selves, and they will go away. He has found a new magic.

This shortcut to transformation will be short lived, unless he can gain additional awareness of the part he observes. Unless the client/seeker develops an awareness of the unit of energy, he or she will not know how to manage it. Even if the observation temporarily drives the subflow of jealousy underground, Bob must be warned that further steps will be required.

Before he will be able fully to handle this jealous aspect, he will have to be able to dive into the energy pool that he labels jealousy and swim around in it. He then will have to learn to climb out of the energy pool, dry off, and observe with awareness what he learned from the swim. That will come in time. For now it is enough to be able to observe.

THE ABILITY TO WAIT

Beyond observing energy, I notice, with the changing of seasons under the magnolia tree, the appearance of something absolutely new—patience. This ability to wait accompanies careful observance and makes it possible. Under the tree it all seems so clear: There is absolutely no need to hurry. In rare moments an energy comes forward in me that is quite unfamiliar; it gently whispers in my ear, "You have nowhere to go, nothing to do. There is time for everything. There is enough for everybody. There is enough for you."

In pushing and hurrying, dignity and power melt away. Along this line a major flaw in the way I practice psychotherapy emerges in my awareness—the arrangement of meeting for fifty minutes once per week with a client. This procedure usually encourages both the therapist and the client to watch the clock. While time boundaries are necessary, I find that it is easy for me to fall into an energy of rushing from one appointment to another. Trapped in this model, I return calls and make administrative decisions in keeping with a fast-food mentality.

Clients are also caught up in this energy and will often rush breathlessly into the session, knowing full well that they have scheduled another event across the city after their therapy interview that will be impossible for them to keep without rushing.

From my shaman friends of the *Ahe-Chay-Cha* and the *Puha Kut,* I have learned that following energy flows is most important, that attuning oneself to the energies of the moment is crucial to transformation, and that such attunement may result in the disturbance of a rigid schedule. In many ways the task of the shaman and the psychotherapist is to disturb patterns. Especially rushing patterns.

A medicine person I know was asked to speak to an organization of psychotherapists. They had him scheduled for a noon meeting of one of their conferences. He showed up at 7:30 a.m., just as they were eating breakfast. The director of the conference scurried over to him and explained that he was early and that they would not have room in the schedule for him to speak until the time he was scheduled, namely noon.

When the conference director had completed his statement, the medicine man replied briefly, "Now is the time I am here. I will not speak at the time you have me scheduled, because now is the time. In order not to disrupt, I will sit quietly under that cottonwood tree over there. Anyone who wishes to converse or work with me will be welcome. I will stay until the Sun goes down."

As I listened intently to the above conversation, I was taken with the dignity and power of this simple man. I canceled the seminar I had scheduled and spent the day under the tree talking with him. I realize that our society is not prepared to operate in this manner at this time; however, I returned to my practice of psychotherapy determined to discover approaches in my work that would allow more flexibility.

Soon, I learned that it worked well for some people to meet weekly for fifty minutes, but for others, who were at another stage of transformation, the meeting time might be two or three hours every other week or once per month. The format didn't matter so much as becoming aware of the hurrying energy that pushed me from one place to the next. Some energy patterns within us need the structure of careful time boundaries; however, other subflows of energy need freedom, more elbow room in relation to the clock.

From my perspective it is the task of the therapist and the client to find contexts for both kinds of energies. To plug all seekers into one formula is a mistake for me, because it deadens both my energy and theirs and because it tends, among other things, to open the way for the inner pusher to dominate the scene.

Under the tree I developed an expanding awareness that I had been dominated by the pusher psychology, so much so that I didn't even know that was what I was doing. Like Marv, I took a hit from the bottle of the pusher, often without knowing it. Push to get out of bed. Push to gobble down breakfast. Push on the freeway. Hurry to the movie to relax, only to stand in line.

Betty has no patience with Bob's jealousy, while Bob has absolutely no patience with Betty's flirtatious aspect, which still insists on popping out even though, by this time, she has broken off the affair. Neither one of them has much patience with therapy: They want a quick fix, because their pain is so intense. Yet the transforming process requires seekers to learn to sit quietly so that they can begin the task of tracking particular energy flows as they lurk in the shadows or surround the ego so tightly that it cannot perceive them as separate entities.

A client who has been on the transforming trail for a while has a dream that comments on her process and also the importance of patience to this process. She tells it in one of our group therapy meetings. In the dream she is back in her childhood home, packing to leave. In her bedroom are many boxes that are mostly filled with bottles. Through a variety of ways her parents detour her from the packing she needs to do in order to leave. The last part of the dream sees her wrapped in a beautiful red scarf, presumably on her way out of the house.

As we discuss the dream in the group, the group members talk about the different images in the dream that appeal to them. My cotherapist associates a ketchup bottle with her dream. A substantial number of us connect strongly with the ketchup bottle, and at first I wonder why. Soon, I observe in myself, as do others in themselves, the obvious interpretation: the ketchup bottle is upside down and symbolizes the impatient self that pounds the bottom of the bottle to get the ketchup out, only to have it make a mess. Patience is called for in using ketchup, and in moving out of the limitations of one's family of origin.

THE SKILLS OF TRACKING

The next quality that emerges from my experiment with the magnolia tree is what a hunter calls *tracking.* With the Native American, waiting promotes tracking, because the hunter first sits, waits, and establishes energetic connection through imaginatively connecting with that which he hunts.

He sees it in his mind first. The hunter and the hunted are not enemies; they are friends, part of the same fabric. They work under the assumption that neither dominates the other; they know instinctively that Nature feeds on Itself. Once the energetic connection takes place they know each other and yield themselves to the process.

The hunter can look for the signs of his game, because he carries in his aware ego a sense of the part of him that is like that which he seeks. This tracking is not limited to creatures we usually think of as alive; it also extends to other energy systems that we usually don't think of as being alive.

Rocks, for example, can be tracked.

Marv, the psychologist, notices a drum in my office and inquires about it; he hears from someone that I am interested in Native American ways and that I conduct monthly sweat lodges. In contrast to Betty and Bob, he discovers an interest inside that he didn't know was there—

the desire to explore himself with me outside the confines of the office in the world of Nature. He ponders his attitude about outdoor activities and notices that he often tells himself that he would like to spend time there but that it is never convenient. Plus, he doesn't like the bugs or sleeping on the hard ground.

I find myself laughing and laughing about a previous time of my life when my idea of camping out, like Bob and Betty's, was a room at the Hyatt Regency. He wonders aloud if I think such a ceremony might help him with his workaholic energy that is out of control. He has located this pusher subpersonality, but he cannot seem to get behind what this energy is protecting. I tell him to start tracking a rock. When he finds this rock, it will be time for him to attend a sweat lodge.

A quizzical look settles on his face, and he asks, "How will I know which rock I am tracking?" I explain to him that something in the rock will reach out to him: maybe the shape, maybe how it lies on the ground, or maybe its color. I remind him of that boyhood experience of walking along a hiking trail when suddenly a stick would strongly invite him to pick it up. Sometimes the stick was for swinging, sometimes for an aid in walking, and sometimes just for companionship.

This experience of tracking a rock was entirely different for Marv, and he would continue it for years. The notion of listening to rocks disrupted his usual approach to reality and opened him to other possibilities. Tracking rocks and listening to them pulled forth aspects of him that had long been crowded out by the inner pusher. These new aspects offered him a new set of energies for relating to his clients. He also retracked his client Rick and his innate ability to allow the woods behind his house to heal him. Maybe, Marv posed the possibility to himself, this connecting with Nature was more than a hypnotic intervention.

THE IMPORTANCE OF DISTINCTION

This tracking self also uncovers *distinction.* One day I sat under the magnolia tree and spotted a white feather with dark bars on it. It looked like a hawk feather, but the more I observed it the more I saw distinctions. On many hawk feathers the dark and white colors were thinner and looked something like a ladder. On this feather the dark and light colors were wider, and the white reflected traces of gold—the marks of an owl. The distinctions were quite subtle, but the birds, while similar in many ways, differed immensely in other ways.

Take other examples—the wolf and the coyote make footprints that are much alike; a baby bear and a coon leave imprints that only the skilled eye can distinguish.

So it is with the tracking of the various subpersonalities within. At first everything looks like a giant ego mass, every aspect enmeshed with every other part. Especially is this true for those of us who grew up in troubled families where boundaries were not well taught. Different and unusual parts were not honored in the family, so we do not honor them inside ourselves.

Now, look at how Betty and Bob use their hunter selves to launch the transforming process. The self-righteous blamer in Bob focuses on Betty's infidelity; this self-righteous energy is so much a part of him that he doesn't know it dominates him. He is so sure he is right about Betty that he believes he knows what is best for her better than she does. Like the enabler in an alcoholic couple, he wants to control what she thinks about other men, because he believes he knows what is best for her to think. As a matter of fact, Betty's use of alcohol careens out of control, although both deny that there is an alcoholic part of her.

This self-righteous attitude, which he developed in his family of origin to defocus his pain from himself to others, has helped him for years. If he spends his energy and time focused on how to improve Betty, he will not have to experience his own pain. At this point in his transforming process, he sincerely believes that all his pain is caused by Betty. He does not yet realize that the pain comes from the interaction of the parts of him that sit at the inner lodge.

When someone asks Bob how he feels, he tells them what he thinks about Betty. His current way of telling the outside world that he hurts is to say, "Betty has committed adultery and trampled on our wedding vows. She has problems—I heard on the radio the other day about sexual addiction, and I think she has a good case of it. She can't control herself." What he cannot see is that the self-righteous part of him is also out of control. He can't stop himself from dwelling on and analyzing his wife.

People in his group point out his self-righteousness and how that energy in him scares them. At first, he doesn't know what they're talking about; it is as if they are speaking Greek. He becomes furious with the group because they won't allow him to tell war story after war story concerning his wife. They tell him they want to know him, and they cannot get to know him if he talks only about his wife and not about himself. At last, he becomes convinced that we are not out to attack him. As he employs a little of his patient self, he hears the sound of self-righteousness in his voice.

By listening to that voice in a variety of ways, he tracks it down through the years as having its origin in his own father, who in turn received that voice from his father. Using the growing skills of his tracking self, he discovers how sickeningly sweet being right is to him and how this pleasure of being right often overrides his interest in genuine contact with others, especially his wife.

While it's hot, this tracking self sniffs out how self-righteous anger assumes that the basis of all communications in marriage is discovering the *right* facts. The observing self notices that, no matter what the situation, the facts always seem to support the self-righteous anger.

Bob reaches a major turning point when one day he turns to his wife and says, "It's hard for me to admit, but I have enjoyed having the goods on you. Or at least a part of me has. That part of me has been largely out of control, and, frankly, I am not sure what I can do about it. Most of me doesn't like that you had an affair, but this one part—and it's quite influential—loved it, because I can hold it over you to try to control things. Plus, I abhor your drinking, yet part of me enjoys helping you after you get drunk. At least then you need me."

Bob is beginning to see a shaft of light between his self-righteous energy and his aware ego, and in this tracking down of the footprints of this subpersonality he develops an increasing distance so he can be more objective. As he becomes more distanced from the intensity of this energy, he actually has a few moments of awareness, made possible by his increasing attitude of observing. Eventually, the observing will lead, as we shall see, to moments of pure awareness, panoramic visions of the person in context. These moments of awareness are then plugged, like new software, into the recovering leader self, the Buffalo Woman, symbol of the aware ego.

THE FEEL OF THE WOOD

Under the magnolia tree I notice, not only the roots, but the twigs and branches that the tree drops. The texture of the wood takes me back to boyhood moments of feeling the smooth texture of a baseball bat and other wood surfaces.

In helping me interpret my interest in the texture of the magnolia tree, a native guide told me about the early training of Lakota children. Before rifles, one of the first skills taught to the Lakota children was the feel of the wood; it was necessary for the making of bows and arrows. They first looked for ash, since it had more spring and was less affected by the weather. Sometimes, though, they would use hickory, cherry, plum, or willow. All the while their hands would be sensitized to the feel of the wood. Something important would pass between the ash sapling and the hand of the Lakota child.

This feel of the wood, still common to cabinet makers and carpenters of all cultures, was integral to hunting skills. Also, they would need the ability to feel the bend of the wood in many of their ceremonies, especially the building of sweat lodges. The magnolia tree awakened in me a growing sensitivity that, in the beginning, had little impact on my life. Like the Lakota children, I had little understanding that the implications of feeling the wood were foundational for future steps on the pathway. Later, the power of the feel of the wood lurched into my psychotherapy office as I met with a client.

One such twig gained my attention one morning; it actually seemed to call out to me. I picked it up and ran my fingers across its surface; the experience sent a charge of alertness through my body. Without further thought I dropped the twig in my pocket. Later that day, I entered into a difficult moment with one of my clients, a moment where the critical father in me bonded with the rebellious daughter in her.

Typically, in these negative bonding patterns, there is little awareness on either side of the transaction, although I often faked awareness to protect myself. Actually, this "faking" of awareness was really an attitude common to many psychotherapists that assumes that the client is the "problem" if there is an uneasy moment in the process. I had been trained in this tradition, and it was an attitude that I usually took, not only in the consulting room but in all my relationships.

I stuffed my hands in my pockets, attempting to escape the discomfort, and there I touched the magnolia twig. With something like an electric jolt, it charged me with its energy. The more I held onto the twig, the more my critical father energy faded into the background. The inner voice, which had been speaking contemptuously of the client in my head, slowly ceased. As the look of awareness dawned in my countenance, my client shifted her consciousness.

As often happens with awareness, the moment transforms into something quite useful. We both now had a sliver of awareness, and I asked her to backtrack with me to the moment that the unease started. Like two skilled hunters we searched for the moment that ignited the negative bonding pattern. When we arrived at that point, we both discovered that we had been feeling vulnerable. We told each other what the vulnerabilities were and experienced a moment of intimacy. At that moment I knew the tree had a spirit/energy capable of calling me toward balance.

A HUNTER HUNTS HER HIDDEN SELVES

One day, as I reflected on how difficult it is to ferret out these hidden inner parts, I crept along a snow-tipped ridge of mountains in Colorado. My partner and spouse, Judith Yost, read to me a myth that startled me in its capacity to summarize the hunter energies (Niethammer, 1977).

Once, there was a very particular maiden who would eat only the white meat from the neck of a buffalo. Whenever she defecated, her feces were white, which she liked. Her mother, worried that her daughter was too thin, slipped some dark meat into her food. After the young woman ate the dark meat, her feces turned black.

Now furious, she taunted them, "Bad feces!"

The black feces felt hurt and angry about her hating them, so they formed themselves into the shape of a man and sprang to life with the notion of gaining recognition. The dung-man dressed himself in fine animal skins and paid a visit to the young woman's father and their tipi, itself adorned in elkhides. The father offered the good-looking man hot stew, but the dung-man, frozen as he was into shape, knew he would melt if he ate it. Soon, the tipi heated up, and so he left before he melted.

As he mounted his horse, the young woman caught a glimpse of him and thought him quite attractive. They exchanged glances and, entranced by new love, she bridled a horse and followed him.

Soon, a warm mountain wind came up and the dung-man began to melt. The girl, tracking him as she was, found one of his otter-skin gloves on the ground filled with feces. Then, she found a moccasin in the same condition. Puzzled, she continued. At last, she caught up with her suitor. He was lying on the ground all melted by the heat, and now in this form she recognized the pile of dung for what it was.

The young woman rode slowly home, humbled as she owned her own darkness, and wailed into the wind, "I have hunted down my own feces."

As we develop the capacity to hunt down the different selves, we next have to find a heat that will melt them down into recognizable form. At just such a time we can turn to Inyan Hoksi, the Stone Boy, who can lead us to a process, the sweat lodge, that will turn up the heat of transformation.

REFERENCE

Niethammer, C. (1977). *Daughters of the earth: The lives and legends of American Indian women.* New York: Collier Books.

4

Purifying the Many Selves

The Stone Boy myth referred to in Chapter 1 narrates the coming of the sweat lodge, *Inipi* in the Lakota language. This sacred purification rite of numerous Native American tribes, even as it is practiced today, provides a lively forum for viewing the transforming process from a slightly different angle—the purifying or clearing of the many selves of sour energy.

A question might arise: how did so many of these selves become sour? The primary or survivor selves—often the critic, pusher, perfectionist, and pleaser that aid in our survival—become stale through overuse. Sometimes they need to be purified of the arrogance they have through dominating us. At other times they need to be purified because they are dead tired through overwork.

In some instances they need to be purified of the anxiety that comes from a subpersonality attempting to pilot the organism without the necessary equipment. These subpersonalities want to run our lives, and then they get in over their heads and panic. It is the panic that needs to drain off and purify.

On the other hand there are hidden selves which we have locked in the cellar because they scare us. Like any living form that is caged, they become sour with the resentment of being ignored, and they then carry the sour rage of not being heard by us. They desire to join the power structure of the personality. As they seep through the permeable boundaries of the ego structure or burst through the locked door, as the case may be, they bring with them toxic energy from their imprisonment. This toxic energy must be handled or it will eventually overcome the organism.

Let us now look at an actual sweat lodge ceremony as a vehicle to understand how the many selves can be cleared of sour energy and thus aid in the transforming process.

THE SWEAT LODGE AS PURIFYING PROCESS

At the edge of the woods crouched a lodge made of shafts of white willow branches lashed together with dime-store twine. Thick ceremonial blankets, tarps, and black gardening plastic substituted for the buffalo hides once used by the Plains Indians. They were layered on the lodge for maximum insulation to provide heat, a necessary element in the purifying process.

On a humid June afternoon the contraption looked hot to me even without heated stones. Since boyhood I had heard about Indian sweat lodges, and I had been invited by one of my Native friends to participate for the first time. He explained to me that there were numerous forms of sweat lodges which varied all the way from a casual social sweat in one's backyard to the rigors of a "medicine" or healing sweat, such as the one we were about to enter.

This explanation helped, because I had visited friends in California, and there people conducted sweat lodges in men's groups and the like who had little or no training in the experience. The pipe carrier further explained that there was certainly nothing wrong with these less informed sweat experiences, but that they were not to be confused with this more powerful process.

He winked and suggested that the white culture might begin marketing prefab sweat lodges to sell with hot tubs as the next item for people who have everything. He convulsed with laughter by the time he got to the punch line: They'll buy it to be cool, and will they be surprised!

The only item that hinted of cool at that point in this experience was my feet, and they were about to get cold. This whole situation looked a little strange and threatening, even bizarre. Extending from the door stretched a meticulously swept path that reached out from the lodge just over ten yards, terminating in the still-roaring fire. Known as *Peta* in Lakota, this fire, the pipe carrier explained, provided the physical and spiritual energy for the process and symbolized the Transforming Energy of the Universe.

Two dozen stones of varying sizes heated in the fire to a glowing hot. Seven yards or so from the door of the lodge, a mound of dirt rose conspicuously, displaying several personal artifacts of the seekers gathered at the lodge. People bring these personal items to symbolize parts of themselves that need purifying. In this way they begin to disidentify with a part of themselves that may have been dominating. For example, if a business person has been driven compulsively by his work, then he might leave his calendar on this mound of dirt, called *Unci* by the Lakota. The calendar then becomes an anchor in his consciousness to prevent his overidentifying with his work.

Twelve or so people, led by the pipe carrier, entered the sweat lodge, crawling clockwise on the ground around a hole that sat in the middle of the lodge until all were in. The pipe carrier situated himself next to the door. One of the seekers slapped at an ant, and the pipe carrier spoke. "Remember the ants were here before you were. I have asked their permission to share this area, and each of you will have to make peace with them." Although I had sat under a tree on and off for several months, I evidently hadn't gotten well enough acquainted with the ants to avoid their bites, pesky as they were.

This guideline highlights the most important aspect of the sweat lodge: All energies are honored inside the lodge, even if they are bothersome inside or outside the person. This approach contrasts sharply with the "noble savage" view of Nature, a view that tends to ignore the aspect of Nature that bites. This Native American approach looks squarely at all the "inconveniences" of Nature and actually magnifies some of them for the purposes of learning.

There is nothing naive about sitting with ants and mosquitoes; their bites puncture superficial idealism. The Lakota word *Inipi* means place of the spirits, a phrase I sometimes translate into my vocabulary as "the place of the energies." Because the ants are bothersome and because I am to honor them, the inference is strong that bothersome inner energies are to be acknowledged, not slapped aside.

Next, the pipe carrier closed the door flap, and it was black inside. The darkness removed the boundaries between the seekers and the rest of the world and taught the benefit of returning to the womb of the True Mother, Grandmother Earth. The person tending the fire on the outside brought in seven rocks to begin with, one for each of the four directions, one for the sky, one for the earth, and one for all living things.

Next, the door closed and the intense sweating began. Was it ever dark! Like a cypress swamp on a moonless night, only more so. I put my finger in front of my face and couldn't see it. The pipe carrier focused the attenton of the seekers first on the Energy (Spirit) of the east. In the east reside connections for parts of self that can see, have insight, maybe enlightenment.

The door opened for more rocks and then closed as the focus shifted to the direction of the south. The south symbolizes the receptor of the north winds. The door opened again for more rocks and then closed as the attention moved to the directon of the west. Since the Sun sets in the west, this direction symbolizes darkness. After we focused our attention on the west, the pipe carrier passed around a metal dipper with a leather handle for us to drink water, what he called Living Water. The leather handle was to protect our hands, because by now it is so hot that a metal handle would burn the hand.

The water came in the nick of time for me, just before panic set in, and I started digging to get out of the lodge for air. The heat itself called forth an aspect of myself that was so completely present with me that I often couldn't see it—the survivor. He was determined to help me survive no matter what.

Also, a touch of the coward showed his face. I don't like to look at him, but there he was, imploring me to dig out. About the time I thought I would make it, the flap dropped again to leave us in complete darkness. This time we focused on the north, Source of the powerful, cleansing winds.

After that the leader passed around the Sacred Pipe for each of us to puff four times in honor of the four directions. The smoke, he explained, carried something from within us that needed to be taken out to the far corner of the Universe where it would be purified and returned in a fresh form. Some other aspects need to go into the earth to be recycled, a process that happened as our sweat dripped on the ground.

Later, we crawled out of the lodge as if being born again, and I lay on the cool ground, my belly button throbbing. It felt as if I were deeply connected with the center of the Earth. Even the hot and humid summer day on the Gulf Coast seemed cool and refreshing as subtle wafts of breezes touched my sensitized body.

THE PURIFYING OF A SUBPERSONALITY

The purifying of a subpersonality, a flow of energy within the person, within the context of a sweat lodge begins when it is called forth through the addressing of a direction. The four directions cover all of the aspects of the personality. Not all of the subpersonalities can be addressed or listened to in one sitting, but the sweat lodge symbolizes the need for the individual to make this voicing of energies a regular aspect of life, often on the moon cycle. A healing sweat lodge is often held as close as possible to the full moon.

Second, the purification takes place through listening to the voice of an energy in a ceremonial community. Not only does the aspect of the person speak out loud, it is also heard by others. And it is heard with little or no judgment. Other people are so busy sweating and attending to the immediacy of the intense experience that they are less critical. The actual physical heat tends to suspend the usual energy of the inner critic and judge.

Some experiments from aboriginal cultures, like eating rattlesnake meat or roasted grasshoppers, I try only once, but this one I would try again and again through the years that followed. After a cycle of seven years of my training with various medicine people, the psychological and spiritual meaning of the sweat lodge dawned slowly on me as a powerful vehicle of the transforming process. In much of my work, I keep it in my mind as a powerful metaphor for purifying myself as I work with clients. Beyond a metaphorical experience, though, I began using the sweat lodge for myself and a few colleagues.

For several years we entered the sweat lodge monthly under the tutelage of a member of the *Ahe-Chay-Cha,* an experienced medicine person or shaman. After this seven year cycle I felt empowered enough to conduct the sweat lodges and other ceremonies myself, and different people began to show up who wanted to experiment with this way of growth.

ATTRACTIONS TO THE SWEAT LODGE

I noticed that Bob and Betty had little or no interest in the sweat lodge when they would hear about it from people in their groups. Sometimes they would process it in the group because they felt competitive or left out, but still, it was not their cup of tea. They would listen in their group process to the voices of group members that were called forth by the sweat lodge experience in the same way that they would listen to any group member's experience. I took care to offer protection from any pressure to attend, because this sort of experience has to be compatable with the unconscious and conscious mind of the seeker.

Marv, the psychotherapist in supervision with me, had a different response altogether from Bob and Betty. He heard about the sweat lodge from other supervisees, and he had a dream about the lodge. He brought this dream to the supervision group for help, and, at the close of the session, inquired about how he could wangle an invitation to attend the sweat lodge.

Like Bob and Betty, he wanted me to know that other than a few camping trips, he had little experience with the outdoors. Unlike them, he felt drawn to try the experience at least once. He explained to me that his feelings were a little hurt, because he had not received an invitation to attend a sweat lodge; it seems he had wanted to attend for some time and had been waiting for me to invite him.

I responded by telling him that most got an invitation by some inner stirring, and that we did not usually advertise sweat lodges to the general public. It was at that time that I gave him the assignment of tracking down a rock that he would bring to lodge. Since our lodge is devoted to a particular kind of medicine power, I, as the chief pipe carrier, ask that a person attend in a supportive role first.

In that way, I explained to him, he could get a notion of what the experience was like before he entered. Interested, but still mostly puzzled, Marv prepared to attend his first sweat lodge. The next week he and I met informally to toss around ideas about how the sweat lodge suggested directions for transformation, some of which follow.

THE HEAT PROMOTES PURIFICATION

Outside the lodge is the fire that heats the stones. Most growth requires the fire—some kind of crisis that shakes the person loose from usual ways of being and doing. Once the energy of the precipitating crisis—marital difficulty, suicidal gestures, hitting bottom with substance abuse, acute depression, phobias, relationship deadends, and the like—subsides, then another kind of heat must come. The fire tender brings in the stones, and the therapist also brings in the stones that heat up the transformational process by slowly calling forth and recognizing subpersonalities that have contributed to the crisis.

Most crises result from a subpersonality or a complex (subpersonalities that have entered into an alliance) taking over the executive function of the person. Through a variety of expressive therapies (intense learning experiences where the many inner selves have a chance to be seen or heard), these subpersonalities come into the awareness of the seeker. The sweat lodge offers an opportunity for many of the selves that have been expressed in traditional psychotherapy to be experienced in greater depth. Then, there are other subflows of energy that are called forth by the primitivity of the sweating and sitting on the ground; they simply will not speak in the office.

Like an uncouth cousin they are too crude for professional offices; they are invited when the person chooses a setting where they are encouraged to come forth. There is something about sitting on the cool Earth, uncomfortable though it is to beginners, that reaches deep into the psyche. Under the conditions of the lodge, it is as if the person returns to the primitive state of sitting on the strong and nurturing lap of the mother. When the flap drops and the dark settles, other energies come forth that harken back to the womb experience.

Through his doctoral work and years of psychotherapy and attending workshops, Marv was well versed with many inner selves. When he finally came to the point of entering our sweat lodge, he heard many voices with which he was somewhat familiar. He watched people crawl out of the lodge, and he processed an anxious voice that he had heard since he was a child. This voice he had analyzed in many ways; it was a voice that screamed in elevators.

Earlier in his life, he had called this voice "claustrophobic." He had analyzed this part of his person as the fear of being entrapped; he had known this aspect in many of his male/female relationships. He felt its vibrations often in his marriage; he noted that he was mostly happy in his marriage but that he was somewhat intimidated by his professionally successful spouse.

As he listened to this frightened voice, he was convinced that he could not enter the lodge. Yet another voice, which wanted to take the risk, also spoke up to him. This voice told him that it would be good for him to learn to face squarely his fear of being entrapped, and that it might help him in his marriage if he could look this fear of being engulfed squarely in the face. After his rock had "found" him, he was prepared to enter, legs shaking. He had heard me share some of these experiences of my first sweat lodge, as well as hearing others, so he was somewhat assured.

In short, just contemplating entering the lodge creates the heat of a crisis that can be in the service of transformation. This induced crisis underlines a profound role of the psychotherapist/shaman in sometimes promoting crisis rather than reducing it. It is not unusual for people who work in this process to comment, "I have enough conflict in the world out there. Why do I need more of it in therapy?" My response usually suggests that the heat has to be turned up to sweat out the toxicity caused by our own rigidity.

THE CEREMONY CALLS FORTH HUMILITY

A most essential subpersonality in this purifying process is the first cousin of patience—humility. Now, mind you, humility also is not a popular contemporary energy; it is mostly disowned in our society. Bookshelves abound in the teaching of the power subpersonalities like self-assertiveness, and rightly so, but you won't find much written or taught about humility. What there is turns my stomach! (he said arrogantly).

Humility in the sweat lodge comes forth with crawling into the lodge wearing little clothing and no jewelry. It is too hot in there for status symbols. Besides, at a certain temperature gold and silver burn the flesh, a factual and metaphorical truth. Crawling along the earth with the tiny creatures, as the leader reminds you that you are a visitor on their turf, is enough to encourage humility.

The first step of the Alchoholics Anonymous twelve-step program is this: "We admitted we were powerless over alcohol (the effects of alcoholism for those who live with alcoholics)—that our lives had become unmanageable." In the lodge and in the program, the beginning step in transformation is the same: to recognize one's powerlessness and to know that the person is out of control when some subpersonality dominates the driver's seat of the personality.

In alcoholism, drug dependence, eating disturbances, and other addictions, the needy child dominates the driver's seat. The mates of alcoholics and the eating disordered usually are dominated by a helping energy that ends up hindering. When people in a twelve-step program say that they are powerless and out of control, they are saying, according to my view, that the leader in them is away without leave. Meanwhile, a power that knows nothing about listening to the other voices seizes the rudder of the ship.

The sweat lodge participants crawl on the ground, and in that way they say that they have lost power to run their lives adequately. Why have they lost power? Because they have lost leadership of themselves. Perfectly good intentions and attitudes within the subpersonalities have become disillusioned and soured through the failure of the human organism to function in its natural way. These subpersonalities that have become soured—some to the point of being demonic—are what need purifying.

After a month of arguing back and forth with himself about what he had seen at his introductory lodge, and after he had run it through his various psychological theories, Marv made the decision to enter. He reminded me of myself some eight years before, only he had more courage. At first, he would later tell me, he was deluged with voices haranguing him about whether he was doing things right, but, as the heat intensified, these voices had their say and quieted down. At first he wondered how he appeared to others in a bathing suit. Did people notice that he was a few pounds overweight? Usually, we talked to each other in office clothes, with our hair carefully combed, but now we looked at each other without our usual trappings. Later, he told me he felt humbled and exposed. So did I each time I entered.

THE WHEEL DISCLOSES THE SUBPERSONALITIES

The wheel inside the lodge discloses what some of the basic energies are and what we are to do with them to purify them of the psychological and spiritual plaque that gathers in their mouths. By *wheel* I refer to the circle inside the lodge whose circumference follows an imaginary line that passes through all of the four directions. In the middle of the wheel sit the heated rocks that steam the participants.

Each of the directions introduces us to the primary selves, the disowned selves, and the unknown selves.

To review for a moment, the primary selves are those inner aspects that have been successful enough for the leader of the inner lodge to have confidence in them, but they tend to overstay their welcome. The disowned selves are those aspects that have been deemed dangerous by the conservative energies. The disowned selves have been banished and, in that state, have soured. They then get together and mount a rebellion. The unknown selves are those aspects that have never made it to the surface of the personality, and some of them feel that they are long overdue.

Throughout this book I will label different primary selves that many of us have. These are just descriptions of generic subpersonalities that tend to have a primary place in running our lives. They are primary in that they dominate the stage of our lives in order to insure survival. The various parts within deserve description idiosyncratic to the reader, so, when I use terms like *the critic,* or *the pusher,* or *the pleaser,* I resort to shorthand language. It will be useful for you to develop evolving descriptions of your inner life that fits your specific inner world.

THE INNER PARTS DISCLOSED BY THE EAST

Inside the lodge the seekers first address the *East* and its energies. In the Eastern domain of our personalities dwell the insight giver, the teacher, the new life giver, the collector of wisdom, positive and his brother hopeful, innocence, delight-over-beginnings, and the pleaser, to name just a few.

To see how a perfectly good energy can go sour, take insight. We all search for insight, and Freud championed the notion that insight was the one ingredient necessary for overcoming neurosis (Freud, 1938). Yet, if we give insight too much power, it will become stiff and inflexible in the form of self-righteous theories. In its sour form it stalks around in the starched collar of self-importance.

Or take the pleaser. The inner pleaser is, in its pure form, a very useful energy, necessary in all intimate relationships. We can better get along with people we love if we know how to please them. Yet this subflow of energy can take over the driver's seat and totally dominate the person. It runs on the fuel of outside approval, and its demands can develop an addiction to approval so great that the person spends twenty-four hour days pleasing with the goal of gaining approval.

Or take the hopeful and positive. Inside the lodge, symbol of any transforming context, people petition for being more positive. Yet, if the inner leader allows the positive complete sway over the person, then the positive sours and turns in denial and delusion. In this soured, even demonic, form, this aspect forms the foundation of all addictions. This is why attempting to use positive thinking as the main tool for approaching an addiction is like throwing the fox in the hen house. When soured, it can become the negative power of positive thinking.

In the case of sexual or other forms of abuse, the young person develops the subpersonality that helps minimize the situation: "This pain is bad but other people have it so much worse." For a child being abused by a parent, this subpersonality helps in survival. To the adult who is attempting to discover the source of the heretofore-unnamed pain, the minimalist inside cannot only be sour but also a block to transformation.

When it came Marv's turn to address the Energy of the East, he did so hesitantly. He later explained that he didn't know whether this was a prayer or what. He had not been in a church for years, and this didn't feel like a church anyway. It also didn't feel exactly like group therapy, since he wasn't talking to anyone in the circle. He was addressing "something" that the pipe carrier had called "the Energy of East," whatever that might be.

He spoke cautiously, searching for something that sounded acceptable, something like, "O Power of the east, help me to have appropriate insight about myself and why I am here." The password that would send the focus to the next person was *metak yeyasin,* but he couldn't remember that, so he just uttered its translation—"all my relatives." Now, he was off the hook for a few minutes.

THE INNER PARTS DISCLOSED BY THE SOUTH

Next, the seekers in the lodge address the *Southern* domain of the person, where dwell numerous wonderful energies. Here rests creativity, receptivity, patience, feelings, nurture, playfulness, flexibility, and the spontaneous, again to name a few. Yet even these valued aspects can sour. This direction invites the honoring of nurture, to cite one example. Nurture in the form of mother energy is essential, yet even nurture can inflate to the point of overpowering the personality. Betty directed her mothering energy to her children and husband, and for years this subpersonality worked well for her.

One day, to her total surprise, she woke up and realized that her children were growing up and that mothering her husband was not sexually interesting. At that point, another energy from the South, playfulness and rebellion, took over. For a while these energies were fun in their pure form, but without proper leadership they, like the mother energy before them, soured.

By this time in the lodge experience, some of the seekers contacted flows of energy within that were vulnerable. Voices broke, and Marv listened intently. It was so dark that he could not see anyone, and he could not always put a voice to people he knew. At that point he did not feel safe enough to express any of his own vulnerability, but he could sense something vibrating inside, something very tender that he had not felt in a long time, something he could not yet put words to, but the heat drew it forth nevertheless. He likened it to times he had participated in Gestalt or psychodrama sessions, only this vulnerability came forward so much easier as the heat intensified.

Later, he went over the stages of development in group situations: the honeymoon phase, the competitive phase, the conflict phase, the harmony phase, and the productive phase. These experiences happened within the group, but the heat seemed to accelerate the process in all dimensions. The stages that took months in group therapy happened much more quickly because of the intensity of the heat.

THE INNER PARTS DISCLOSED BY THE WEST

The next direction of the Medicine Wheel is *West.* Since the Sun sets in the West, it reminds us of death, completions, good-byes, and grief. Most powerfully, though, it calls to our attention darkness, the shadows that lurk around the inner lodge. At this point in the sweat lodge, the pipe carrier will sometimes invite people to allow whatever voices that usually are repressed to speak. Since, by this time, it is so hot that people have ceased to censor as they usually do, and since it is totally dark, they often will let voices from within speak that maybe they have never heard. These disowned or even unknown voices will say things that totally surprise them.

In the course of psychotherapy or some other profound learning process, there comes a time when these disowned personal aspects have to be faced. They are the inner dragons that we carry with us, and following chapters will pay close attention to them. For now, it is enough to say that the heat of the transforming process loosens them up, and they float to the surface.

On this particular day the pipe carrier invoked those aspects of the person that were inarticulate. Marv listened with astonishment as he heard roars of anger, shouts of joy, loud laughter, sobs, and other utterances. He opened his mouth, but nothing would come out. Something from down deep wanted to be expressed, but, like the dry heaves, nothing came out.

Even so, he felt loosened up by the free expressions of others. Since it was so dark, he felt no intrusion into anyone's space. Normally, he would have felt some embarrassment over such spontaneous eruptions. He wondered what could be done with all of these impulses pulsating within the lodge? A conservative voice within cautioned him about the advisability of the jungle-like voices roaming around without proper professional guidance.

THE INNER PARTS DISCLOSED BY THE NORTH

The next direction is that of the *North,* and it discloses a beginning map of what to do with these powerful disowned and unknown energies when they make their appearances. The medicine wheel knows that the rush of energy that comes from the repressed selves coming out in the West will need direction. It also provides us with a clue in managing those survivor energies who are so well known that they overwhelm us and who would love to return to repressing the energies that have been loosed out of the West.

The North is the direction from which the North Winds blow. To the Native American, these winds clear out humidity (and now pollution), bring rain, and provide strength. This direction symbolizes the thrusting, pushing, striving, organizing, objective, disciplined, controlled, managing, impersonal, and rational, again to name a few. These subselves can be useful, but they also can become so dominating that they get stale. They can become power-mad and suppress primitive parts of the person, as Betty did with her playfulness and sexuality. They can get confused and try to control and discipline other people rather than focusing on their job with the inner person, as with Bob. In this state they overwork themselves and lose energy for the organism.

Yet in the heat of the transforming process these Northern energies usually start to shrink (or with some people, enlarge) to their proper size. They then become allies with the purified protector/controller and help the aware ego in managing these newly discovered and uncovered aspects of self that are emerging in the transforming process.

In the sweat lodge the Northern Energies are honored, but they are balanced out by the Southern Energies of vulnerability, feeling, and celebration. In Greek mythology the Northern Energy is Apollo, and the Southern Energy is Dionysius. In Eastern religion the Northern energies are Yang, and the Southern are Yin. When these energies work together, life flows naturally as the energies are balanced through the aware ego. When the person overidentifies with one to the neglect of the other, then the souring and blocking takes place.

The sweat lodge circle had now been completed for the first time with Marv, and he now felt at home with these Northern energies. They sounded more rational to him, more organized, as he was accustomed to. He also felt relieved to hear people who apparently had lost it during the South and the West come back to their "senses." He explained it later as a time when people could reconstitute their defense mechanisms; such a reconstitution was necessary for him on that first day.

That night he would dream profound dreams that had been stirred by this experience. The following week he would process himself in a way that brought new energy to his work as a psychotherapist. He felt stronger and, at the same time, more vulnerable. He could join his clients more readily in their pain but not get trapped in it. In short, he was more in balance with his life, and he was convinced that he had found an "answer" that would make him feel somewhat like this from that time on.

It wasn't long, to his considerable disappointment, until the imbalances began to creep in again. About the time he felt he was back to where he was before he ever entered the lodge, it was the full moon again and time to enter once again. He was learning that, on this pathway, no matter how evolved people are, they cannot escape oscillating between balance and imbalance. The sweat lodge purification rite is there to help restore balance and harmony with the natural flows of the world.

CONCLUDING REMARKS

So much material emerges in the powerful metaphor of the sweat lodge that it is easy to overload. It might be helpful to return to the more linear aspect of the person for a brief review of how the purifying of the many selves occurs.

1. The directions of the medicine wheel point to the truth that selves tend to form alliances or complexes: They group together in certain functions of the personalities.
2. Some groupings of selves are overworked. They aid in helping the person survive but become stagnant through overuse. They can be purified by being smoked out into the open so they don't dominate the personality. The sweat lodge points to the need to smoke these dominant selves out into the open where they can be seen. The initial stages of psychotherapy are, according to my view, the smoking out of these energies so the person can begin to disidentify from them. The contamination of domination begins to drain off; hence, a feeling of purification.
3. As awareness develops of these primary selves, the ego space now has more room. It is no longer dominated and has the advantage of growing awareness. In this purified condition the ego space is now more willing to listen to the hidden selves. Not only is the aware ego more willing, it also is more capable of managing these energies. *As the awareness grows in the ego space, the subpersonalities lose more and more of their toxic quality and thus are purified.*
4. Historically, other groups of selves fall out of favor with the executive function of the person and sour because they are ignored. Again, they can be "sweated" out into the open where they have a chance to voice their discontent. In voicing their discontent, they complain, even rage, at their repression. They must have their day in court, and when they do, they tend to quiet down and bring new emphases to the organism.
5. As these hidden selves come out into the open, they tend to balance out the survivor or primary selves that have dominated the scene. However, they do not balance out the other energies automatically. The aware ego acts as a balancing agency by channeling first one and then the other energy into a situation. The seeker may need the help of both therapist and shaman in balancing these flows of energy that have been brought forth by the sweat lodge experience. Some of these voices are of a coarse nature and need more civilized voices to balance them out; however, they are full of energy and juice. They can, if balanced with awareness, provide the seeker with the spice of life for which so many of us search.
6. The rigors of living on this planet are such that this purifying and balancing need to take place on a regular basis.

REFERENCE

Freud, S. (1938). *The basic writings of Sigmund Freud* (A.A. Brill, Ed.). New York: The Modern Library.

5

The Visionary Selves

Growth moves in spirals.

In the early spirals people notice that they are a variety of parts. As they come around again, they discover the bipolar nature of these parts—the dynamic tension found in these parts that will occupy our attention in the next chapter. Each time they travel around the spiral staircase, it looks as if they are in the same place.

In the psychotherapy process they may well say, "This is terrible: I'm back where I started." On another point in the transforming spiral, seekers offer this objection to the therapist/shaman: "I have all of this awareness of different aspects of myself, but how come my problem is not solved? How come, for example, I haven't found the person to spend the rest of my life with?"

At that time a wider vision is called for, one that can enable seekers to catch a glimpse of the whole and of hitherto hidden parts, where they have been, where they are going. This vision will disclose that they are hiking on a staircase, moving upward, even though they appear to be at the same place. It will disclose that developing awareness offers the person many more choices about problems but does not always "solve" every problem on the horizon. It will show that the person gains more inner software at every turn of the spiral if there is awareness, but that this new software is not a free ticket from pain or from negative bonding patterns.

After nearly two years in therapy, Bob had acknowledged the jealous aspects of himself and experienced the sad parts that had been ignored when his father died some twenty years before. He no longer focused so much on Betty, and their marriage improved. Despite this progress he lashed out in a group therapy session, "This therapy is crap—my mother sneezes a thousand miles away, I feel guilty. Here I am forty-one, and I still don't know who I am. Well, that's not exactly true. I truly can recognize the little boy in me when I talk to her, and other parts as well. But when I feel jealous and angry with Betty, I run it into the ground with her. It makes things worse. What I wish is that the central office inside of me worked better. I feel betrayed by the group; I should be getting better faster."

BEGINNING VISIONS

The task of the psychotherapist is at this point to facilitate a wider vision of the process. In Bob's case the process moved much slower because, at first, he was not open to move outdoors with his work, where the eye physically would not be limited by the four walls of the office. He traveled from home to auto, to office, and to health spa with as little contact as was possible with the physical climate. His vision was limited by walls and climate control; physical space truly did dictate function. Just as the outer eye becomes dulled by the limitations of the four walls, so does the inner eye. No matter how symbolic an indoor space is, it is no substitute for the Natural world of the outdoors.

It was precisely at this point that should a client be receptive, a consultation by a shaman could offer a quantum leap in the process. In Bob's instance, he showed no interest in Native American ways; they seemed "too hokey." In lieu of that, I listened carefully for references in our sessions with some connection that he might have with the Natural world outside the usual cubicles in which he lived, worked, and played. As in other features of the therapy process, I waited for such references to arise naturally from the life of the seeker.

Finally, Bob moved outside enough to notice his backyard for the first time in years. When he first moved into his home, he had worked in the yard and gotten his hands in the dirt. Soon, his growing professional practice pushed him to hire out that job. Without realizing it, he had slowly distanced himself from the yard because it only represented more work on weekends already devoted to overtime in his practice. On the back fence line of his yard sat a magnificent catalpa tree, a tree whose leaves seemed as large as an elephant's ears. Although Bob had lived in this house for fifteen years, he had never really paid attention to the tree, except that he knew it added value to the resale of the house.

When he casually brought this noticing up in our session, I suggested that he talk to the tree when he felt his jealously come forward. If I had not had an association with a magnolia tree, I would not have registered this beginning vision on his part. Therapists who are not well connected with Nature do not notice when other living creatures offer to help facilitate the process. This notion of other living creatures being essential to the transformational process is a crucial one, and I will develop it in later chapters.

Bob found this quite easy to do and soon addressed the catalpa as "Mr. Tree." He made it clear, on the other hand, that he would not tell about this exercise either in group or at the office. Children will often talk to their pets when they feel angry or hurt with their parents, and Bob found that he could do this quite naturally, since he had talked with his dog as a small boy about the problems in his family. These tree talks became his version of a vision quest. Something about connecting with a living entity other than a human opened up patience for him to continue the journey. Betty also felt relieved that he found "someone" else to share his anxiety with besides her. Later, when his anger about her affair would finally come to the surface, his conversations with Mr. Tree became essential.

At those times, he felt like becoming physically violent with Betty. His rage erupted when it finally came to the surface, and he found through our couples meetings that it worked for him to leave the field of interaction with his wife at those times and go out to the tree. By first hitting a punching bag and then holding onto the tree, the rage seemed to pass. The tree acted as an anchor that kept him from spouse abuse and in some way recycled the rage into more manageable anger. Like me before him, he hoped that his neighbors did not notice him talking to and holding onto the prodigious tree.

Meanwhile, Marv too had been having beginning experiences with living creatures other than humans. He noticed time and again that spiders showed up in his house. In supervision he mentioned them as pests but also wondered if they had some symbolic value. When he talked of these creatures entering his consciousness, I knew that he was moving closer to the point of embarking on a vision quest, because I had had similar experiences that prepared me for my first Native American vision quest.

In the months preceeding my first vision quest, I also had noticed any number of birds that came to my backyard and sat on a large pecan tree. Had they been there all along and had I just not noticed them? At the time I couldn't fathom the meaning that these encounters with the birds had, any more than Marv could when he experienced these beginning visions with spiders. These encounters provided the entry into living encounters that were to come on a more intentional vision quest. As we shall see, they were the warm-ups before the action to follow.

THE INTENTIONAL VISION QUEST

The Native American vision quest offers a wide-angle lens for us to look at the transformational process, especially the point on the spiral that requires a larger vision. It is the quintessential mythological act, a sign stimulus of the first order that releases energy. My experiments in personal growth carried me into several such vision quests guided by Native American medicine people, and I have found them to be a paradigm for more informal visions quests in psychotherapy and other growth endeavors, such as this one that Bob had in his backyard.

Focusing on the vision quest as a metaphorical act is not necessarily a suggestion for the seeker to engage in a quest exactly like the one that follows. For some it fits the Larger Plan, and for others it doesn't. Primary to the transformational journey is discovering myths that appeal and tickle the inner life; these Native American myths, ceremonies, and learning experiences appeal to me because they are congruent with my primitive self and also question my urban world-view.

People like Bob and Betty long for a restoration of the primitive in their lives at an unconscious level, but their awareness is not yet prepared for this particular experience. It is my view, however, that therapist and seeker must find some avenue for reconnecting the seeker with the Natural Order if the process is to reach the primitive depths necessary for profound transformation.

After months, sometimes years, of preparation, the seeker of visions journeys to a wilderness area, usually with a support group. After a period in the sweat lodge, he goes alone with pipe or medicine stick in hand to a vision area. On my first vision seeking, *hanblecheyapi* in Lakota, I was instructed by my Indian guide to fast from food and water for at least two days, maybe four. At the time, I was teaching a seminar at a local medical school, so I asked a colleague who was a physician about the medical advisability of such a fast. He emphasized that going without water and food for four days was not only medically unsound but also outrageous. He further advised me not to mention my plans to any other colleagues, for obvious reasons.

My guide laughed and laughed when I told him of this advice, telling me, "Someday you will know your body well enough to go four days without food or water, as we do. But this is okay: you can begin here."

To be safe, I bootlegged a banana as well.

At this point my inner parts that were most evident to me were the primary or survival selves. They were agitated: asking me why I was doing this to myself, looking for ways out of the situation, pushing me, telling me what I should do, complaining that I wasn't doing it right, criticizing me for not knowing more Indian lore, and, finally, emphasizing that I didn't know how to take care of myself, else I wouldn't be in this situation.

You might recognize these voices as being the same ones that gave me a hard time about the risk of involving myself in the sweat lodge. They are my conservative voices, and they watch out to see that I don't take unnecessary risks.

The sweat lodge that launches the vision seeking is often three or four times as intense as the usual *inipi,* so I was quite weak by the time I reached the top of the mesa I had selected for my vision spot. Once there, I drew a circle in the dirt, perhaps ten feet in diameter. Outside the circumference of the circle, I placed a line of brightly colored pouches filled with sacred plants. This line of energy was there to protect me from any energy that shouldn't be in the circle. Then, inside the circle, I set up the medicine wheel with a color flag at each of the ordinal directions. In the middle of the circle, I placed a green flag for the earth and a blue flag for the sky.

Then I sat down with nothing to do for forty-eight hours, not even eat or drink. I felt frightened, and realized I had become something of a human *doing* rather than a human *being.* The inner pusher, active as he is in the city, fairly buzzed in the background, since he had nothing to push me to do in this setting.

I selected an area with no shade, because it was cold when I arrived. As a cold front passed, the temperature rapidly rose. The sun beat down. The first widening of my vision was that of connecting with my body in a new way. I listened to my stomach rumble; I tasted the dryness in my mouth; I felt my muscles and bones as I slept on the ground. With nothing to do but sit, I looked at the aging spots on my hands and listened to the sound of my own breathing. I was getting acquainted with my physical self.

The hotter the sun grew and the drier my mouth got, the more vulnerable I felt. The first visions were those from childhood. Inner aspects long forgotten, even actively disowned, crawled across my consciousness like the wounded animals they were.

During one particular vision seeking (I would go on a series through the years), I suddenly recalled moments of childhood trauma not uncovered in years of my own previous psychotherapy. Over the next months, these traumatic incidents clamored to voice and vision themselves to me. Stripped, with few or no clothes, no food or water, little covering except a blanket or sleeping bag, the seeker automatically becomes vulnerable. Since the executive self has chosen to put the organism in a vulnerable spot, the vulnerable selves come forth. Later, we will look closer at these vulnerable aspects.

After a dark night on the ground, the sense of dread and possible death left me, and I noticed living creatures in my medicine circle. I addressed them as *mitakuye oyasin,* a Lakota phrase that translates "all my relatives." The more I fasted and sat alone, the more I acknowledged my connection with these creatures. I just hung out there with them as part and parcel of the countryside, and, strangely, they seemed to recognize and accept me. Sometimes when outdoors, I felt isolated, helpless, a foreigner from the lands of glass-enclosed air conditioning. Like Bob, I had become a person detached and alienated from the Natural world.

Not this morning that I describe here. As I moved toward a waking state, I sensed something drawing near. Without opening my eyes, I reached for the hunting knife I had stashed under my bedroll. The presence grew stronger and stronger, along with an unusual sound, one totally foreign to me.

My eyes opened to focus on a hummingbird that darted across my vision. The bird moved toward me until it hovered immediately in front of my face, as if it was attempting to tell me something, and then slipped away with astonishing speed. Tears of happiness flowed; then I sobbed uncontrollably.

I asked myself, "Why?"

That I was known and fully accepted by this Sacred Place pounded with every beat of the hummingbird's wing—definitely a mythical, not logical, experience.

Later, when I surrounded this experience with words and ideas, I recalled a description by the anthropologist Gregory Bateson. He described the Native American rain dance not so much as an effort to bring rain as to affirm the Indian's oneness with the Universe (Bateson, 1979).

The hours passed; the sun was relentless. Off in the distance, I saw large cranelike birds walking through marshes. Since I was in southern Colorado, I knew that I was hallucinating. They walked with grace, inviting me to walk with them. This vision, and others, disclosed spiritual parts of myself, sources that merit further discussion in the chapter on spiritual selves.

What followed was a series of hallucinations and experiences that brought a variety of winged creatures into my consciousness. A mountain bluebird stayed with me the whole time I sat in my circle. Even when I returned to the base camp, the bird appeared to me time and again.

As I drove toward the airport, a bluebird still came into my vision. Other experiences too tender for recording here happened to me. I returned to the base camp to talk with a shaman about my experiences.

THE GIFT OF A NEW NAME

Back in camp I sat under a tree with a shaman. He listened to my experiences and offered some interpretations. Mostly, though, he listened intently. When I concluded, he spoke. "Your new name for this stage of your journey will be *Fuswah Enhaleswah,* which can translate as Winged Medicine." I was impressed with his ability to name me, and it also staggered me to think of the responsibility of a shaman to name the person.

Many years later, when I became the chief pipe carrier and shaman for a vision quest, I would see that the shaman does *not* do the naming. The Environment of the Mountainside does the naming; this complex set of relationships that we call the Local Environment is an expression of the Divine that offers the name. The Lakota name for the Divine Energy that is present is called *Tunkashila,* or Rock Energy. Symbolically, this Divine name describes a basic Energy that arises from the interaction of person within a Natural context.

In the interaction the Landscape sends certain experiences, as I described above, and these visitations from the other living creatures do the naming. The shaman simply notices the name that has been given; the gift of noticing and seeing the name is important. As a shaman in a vision quest, I feel little or no weight of responsibility, because the vision is not given by me. I simply notice what has been given and voice it.

Within two years Marv felt prepared to participate in a one-day vision fast. He had noticed his awareness of living creatures being heightened. He had been sweating with me on a monthly basis during this time, and he wanted to take this further step on the pathway. Many creatures visited him during his quest, but his attention kept returning to the spiders in the trees near his vision circle. They spun intricate and beautiful webs in the trees. In the morning when he awakened, he felt his attention drawn to that area. The dew of the morning reflected the sun through the web in such a way that he was mesmerized as the tiny water droplets revealed mysterious worlds.

He watched with fascination as the spider near him waited for small insects to fly into the web. In time a small moth did just that. The sight of the spider feeding on the moth caused him to flinch, because there was so little primitivity in his life. At first, it seemed cruel to him, and he raged at the spider, tempted to tear down its web. Then, that feeling settled down as the day progressed. Later, the creature ventured into his circle and crawled up on his hand. He wasn't sure what kind of spider it was, but he allowed it to sit there.

At times as he looked at the creature, he felt an urge to smash it, yet another impulse of tenderness came to him. These opposing inner energy flows built a firm bridge between him and the tiny insect. Like me and the winged ones, he sensed that this crawling creature was a representative of the larger order of Nature stating that he was accepted. He was no longer an outsider in this hillside environment. The feeling of belonging penetrated to the depths of his heart, because it seemed to be unconditional. He certainly had done nothing to earn it except sit there without food and very little water. In a profound way he was being reclaimed as a creature of Planet Earth. His intent in being there was not to dominate or control but simply to join. Grandmother Nature honored this intent.

On this same vision quest a woman, a Chickasaw, used this venue to return to her roots. As an executive in a large corporation, she had become alienated from the genetic code of her ancestors that pulled her toward a respect for all that lives. As she sat in her circle just far away enough from Marv that she could not see him, she watched carefully as a skunk approached her. It seemed unconcerned about her because she was just sitting there quietly. She considered throwing a rock at it. Then she recalled my instructions to first attempt to establish an energetic connection with the creature before acting hostile. Her protector selves gave her permission to try looking the skunk in the eye for a few moments before she bolted in fear. And try she did.

The skunk ambled closer and finally walked, not only into her circle, but right up on her chest. Although she had some fear, she had mostly interest and acceptance, something she felt reciprocated from the skunk. After a time, the skunk left without spraying her or the area. She later told me that the only reservation she had during the whole experience was that I would name her "Skunkwoman."

Marv hankered after an experience with a wolf, cougar, or hawk, but here he was spending his time with a tiny spider. As one of the pipe carriers in charge, I was reluctant to give him the name "Son of Spider," yet that was what the Sacred Mystery of the Earth and Sky had given him. Who was I to argue?

Later, I would remember a myth told me by a grandfather about how the Sacred Mystery used the spider to create the universe. *Wakan Tanka* had a spider on His/Her shoulder and ordered the spider to jump into space. As the spider jumped into space, it took a strand of its web with it. Then it jumped again. From this tiny web, the universe began.

So it was that Marv received the gift of an important name; it was paradoxical. In our culture the spider is seen as a pest. In the culture of the Earthwalkers, the spider was viewed as the creative partner of the Divine. Later it would dawn on him that the essence of the spider is knowing how to wait for its food. This energy to wait, symbolized and brought forth by the spider, would help balance out Marv's out-of-control pushing energy.

THE PHYSICAL SELF AWAKENS

Another feature of the visionary selves is that they reveal the importance of the physical or bodily self. A principal reason for the failure of many major religions and usual psychotherapies, according to my view, is that they have ceased to impress the bodily self. They, in fact, often seem to be antiphysical in nature. Any process of change that does not involve the physical self is doomed to stagnation, and it follows that one of the first orders of business in the transformational process is to get the attention of the body.

When people complete a vison fast, they and their bodies know they have been through something profound. The same is true for an experience in psychodrama, or some other deeply expressive therapy. The first time I went through a three-hour psychodrama at the Moreno Institute in New York City, I knew that I had participated in a new birth of personal and interpersonal energy. I was sweating, crying, and out of breath. That night, when I lay down in bed, I felt like I had been through a running marathon.

Whatever form of transformation people choose, they must demand the attention of their physical selves. The very bodily tissue must be involved or the change will be superficial. For this reason we often invite our clients to engage in some form of body work—such as Rolfing, sweat lodges, or massage—while they are in the course of psychotherapy.

Marv noticed right away that his time on the hillside forced him to experience his body in a different way. To begin with, the sweat lodge before the vision quest was such that he lost a large amount of bodily fluid. Yet, as he sat in his circle, he soon felt the urge to urinate. He wondered about that. Where was the urine coming from, since he had lost so much bodily fluid? He made a note to check it out when he returned to civilization. Early the next morning, he felt the urge for a bowel movement. He had forgotten toilet paper, but he soon found a position in the woods that was comfortable. He would later say that this was the first time in his life that he felt natural with his bodily eliminations. Like the woman in the myth, he had literally followed his feces.

His inner organs, he explained, seemed to appreciate the time off he gave them through his fasting. This instance was, in fact, the first time ever he had given them twenty-four hours without having to do their usual work. His nose ran, and he had no Kleenex. Yet, that seemed very natural as well. Furthermore, he felt like spitting. He had not spit since he was a kid, when he used to have contests with his best friend. One way he passed time was to spit at different leaves. Later, when he talked with me about it, he would comment that now we could add "spitting therapy" to our list that included "tree therapy."

Another emission of bodily fluid that came to his mind was ejaculation. He didn't do that, but somehow he felt that this experience with the other bodily fluids would help him enjoy that experience more. Plus, the very sensuality of this experience made him feel virile in a way that was beyond his norm.

Marv noticed that, when he was accessing different subpersonalities on the vision quest, they would be hungry for different foods. His survivor wanted fruit; his deprived child wanted Twinkies or pancakes; his warrior wanted red meat. As a result of his experiences and others as well, we at our clinic formed new hypotheses about eating disorders.

This area is fertile for research: some subpersonalities may be out of control, for example, with sweets, while others are out of control with salt. It is not enough, according to our hypothesis, to notice what one eats or even what is the function of the eating; one must also notice "who" does the eating, which subpersonality impulses the eating. When carefully listened to by the aware ego, these subpersonalities often lessen the intensity of their demands.

THE INTRODUCTION OF VULNERABLE ENERGIES

One of the more important developments of the vision quest is the induction, or pulling forward, of vulnerable energies by the experience. Many aspects of the person that have been deeply wounded go into remote hiding after the wound. It is quite difficult for the seeker to discover what the tender vibration is in the background. A sense of anxiety, of pain, filters up to consciousness, but what sends it often remains a mystery to both seeker and therapist.

The vision quest is a powerful approach to these vulnerable energies. I hypothesize that they feel supported by the countryside in such a way that they are willing to come into the consciousness of the seeker.

For me, this was powerfully true. For most of my life, I had experienced a sense of anxiety over something, but I did not know what it was. A few weeks after the vision quest that I described above, I felt the urge to talk to a family member about my childhood. Without knowing exactly why, I flew to my sister's home in Maryland. While we were discussing matters about our childhood, I suddenly had a flash of an experience where I was severely abused by my grandmother while my parents were out of town.

The energy from this experience had been lodged deep in my psyche, and it was reluctant to come forward until I had sat on the hillside. Something about sitting on the lap of our Grandmother, the Earth, allowed this experience, with the help of a family of origin visit, to come forward. The shaman had done his job in helping jog this energy loose, and it became the job of my psychotherapist at the time to help me learn how to take care of that wounded self.

TRANSFER OF PARENTING AND AUTHORITY

Sitting on Grandmother Earth's lap brings to mind one of the principal features of the vision quest—the transfer of parenting. The vision quest is a metaphorical act of the moving of the human from his or her family of origin to the larger family of adult humans. In the Native American tribes the seeker left the extended family and went out alone to sit and fast. In this way there was an actual transfer of authority from the parents to the Grandparents—Earth and Sky.

In this tradition the seeker continues to acknowledge and respect the actual mother and father, but the deeper authority now moves between the adult and the Nourishing Source of all on the planet, Earth and Sky. A by-product of the vision quest is the clarification of this boundary between the generations. It will often act as a healer of the boundary disturbances that are so evident in dysfunctional families.

This process aids enormously in codependent behavior, where an adult relates to an important other out of a needy subpersonality such as the scared little boy or little girl rather than out of the aware ego. As seekers establish a link between themselves and Nature, there emerges an opening so that the bountiful nourishment of Nature can flow into the individuals. As they recognize their abject dependence on Nature as a whole, they become more appropriately dependent in intimate relationships.

Marv brought a case for supervision just after he returned from his vision quest. His client, Laura, had been seeing him for over a year. She had come to him because she was depressed, crying, and unable to sustain ongoing intimate relationships. Her mother had died when she was a teenager, and she had, in effect, become the surrogate spouse of her father, an alcoholic. The boundary between the spouse subsystem of the family and the offspring subsystem had been severely disturbed in this way for years, but the death of the wife/mother amplified the disturbance.

Laura was desperate for nurturing because she had had her mothering interrupted, and she had had little substance in her fathering because she was parenting her own father. Each time she began a promising relationship with a man, it would abort when her needy little girl would burst forth without any channeling through the aware ego. This little girl would cling to the man, and it would scare him away.

In other instances she would attract men who attempted to engage her inner mother through their deprived inner little boys, who functioned outside their awareness. She would break up with these men because she had already spent a large portion of her life mothering her own father. Why would she want more of this?

When Marv returned from his vision quest, he had a new energy about him. He no longer related to her through his over-responsible father. He had been doing this for months, and they had in fact been locked into a negative bonding pattern in the therapy process. His responsible father would suggest things for her to do, and she would feel resentful but afraid to say no. She would do what he said, but pout about it and withdraw from the process of therapy by being late or missing appointments.

Now he sat with her equipped with new awareness. Through the power of his new awareness of his over-responsible father, he broke free of the negative bonding pattern. Comforted by his new awareness, she launched into a grieving process concerning her mother that now reached a nodal point. She was just about ready to transfer the power from her dead mother to herself, but she didn't know how. Neither did Marv, and that was the question he brought to supervision.

The supervision team suggested that he go with Laura to her mother's grave for a further voicing of the aspects of herself that were fixed on grieving. Once at the grave, the supervision suggestion went like this: Marv could facilitate a transfer of authority in parenting from Laura's mother to Mother Earth. Having just returned from the profound experience of his vision quest, Marv jumped at this suggestion as one that might help.

At the grave Laura spent time by herself saying something to her mother that she had wanted to say for years. Having concluded with that, she motioned for Marv to join her. They sat in the remote cemetery on a cool, early spring day. Puffs of clouds whisked across the sky as the wind blew from north to south. A mother mockingbird worked assiduously on her nest; a rabbit nibbled at the corner of the mother's gravestone. They talked about the support they received from sitting on the ground, about the rest they received by looking at the mockingbird build the nest, and about the general sustenance of that place.

Marv asked Laura if she was ready to become a daughter of the Earth and leave her biological mother to rest there. An affirmative energy came forth, and she had turned an important corner on the spiral.

VISIONS DISCLOSE RELINQUISHING ENERGY

Next, the visionary selves open the way for a process known as relinquishing, *en-see-zom-kosee* in the Creek language. Relinquishing is something like the process known as detachment in the twelve-step programs, only more so. The heat of the sweat lodge and the solitude of the vision fasting symbolize the necessary intensity of experience in one part of the self letting go of its hold on another part.

Often clients will comment, "I am not ready to let go of the protection and control that I need. I know I want to get to the wounds of the inner child, but I am afraid. I am not ready to let go and allow these energies to come through."

At times like these a particular brand of visionary self is needed—a willingness to let go, even though the time may not be now. Willingness precedes relinquishing. Willingness is what enables a person to continue on the transformational journey when nothing else helps. There may be no hope, no progress, no commitment, and little feeling, but if there is willingness, the journey continues.

Marv's client, Laura, had experienced this process. During the years following her mother's death, her protector selves had held on tightly to the key that kept her grief locked up. They would not allow her to experience the deep sadness, because they were afraid that the grieving energy would inundate her consciousness. At this point, "they" were Laura as Laura knew herself. Yet included in their midst was a subpersonality called "willingness." She was willing to be more open, even though she could not actually be open to her vulnerability in a conscious way; it was this willingness that brought her to therapy and allowed her to go to the grave with Marv.

Because of the careful work Marv and Laura had done with her primary or protector energy, these protector selves were willing at the grave to loosen their grip on the deep wounds, not only of her mother's death but the pain caused from the boundary disturbance in her family.

This letting go of the protector selves of their imprisonment of the hidden selves is the experience of relinquishing. Once this relinquishing occurs, then the transforming process is in full gear. It is the relinquishing that allows the seeker to let go and enter into a subpersonality and experience the full range of feelings. It is this letting go that marks most turning points in transformational work.

VISIONARY ENERGY UNITS AND MOONCYCLES

Before I leave our discussion of the visionary selves, I want to direct the attention of our dialogue to the human body, particularly the female body, as a source of visionary energy. Many practices in the shaman's domain require balance *(demo-bo-kosee)* of the male and female energies. A shamanistic tradition holds that a male shaman cannot transform himself into an animal creature for the purpose of healing unless he closely links with a female shaman, sometimes his spouse.

I certainly have found this to be the case, and I draw on the energy of my spouse, Judith Yost, both in the sense of the balance of these energies and also in her being a source of teaching. We act as teachers to each other, and I rely on her teachings in this area to underline the natural functions of the body as a source of visionary energy. As a pipe carrier in her own right, she works with women in our "tribe" by enabling them to honor their menstruation as a source of visionary energy.

When Betty brought up the experience of her daughter's first period and how she felt about it, Judith pointed out that the first period for a woman, the menarche, is a powerful time when she can gain a vision of what it means to be a woman. It is as if the body calls the seeker, mother and child, to open the third eye while the body itself opens up to new possibilities of fertility and creativity.

Judith also teaches that women who enter the transforming pathway tend to tune their periods to the moon cycle. The tendency to align with the natural order often locates the woman's period near (say, within seven days) the new moon. Over a period of time, women who join together in a tribal coherence will then menstruate on the new moon and enter the sweat lodge with men on the full moon, though this practice is not always followed.

Sometimes, a woman embarks on a special experience in a "moon lodge," where she can sit alone on a hillside or in a small tent or hut to open herself to the Sacred Mystery as her body opens itself. The body feels honored when the person listens closely to its cue as to when to sit for a brief vision.

During this time she can "see" things she cannot ordinarily see. In ancient times, the male shamans would process these visions had by women during the moon lodge experience and then interpret them in the larger tribe. These visions were greatly valued as the unique contribution of the feminine. This practice stands in sharp contrast to our culture's notion that a woman is useless during this time and that she should medicate herself and zone out until the whole distasteful experience is completed.

Rather than seeing menopause as a loss of fertility, the pipe carrier energy in Judith teaches that it is a time for women to enter a Grandmother lodge, a monthly time for opening up to visionary energies that continue to be released by the moon cycle but without the bleeding. What women can see at this time is to be greatly honored for their own lives and for the life of the tribe. Naturally, the women in our work are children of our culture and therefore have parts of themselves that rage against menopause and Grandmother energy. This visionary teaching offers another pole of energy and opens up new possibilities.

As a male psychotherapist/shaman, for me this teaching opens the importance of tuning the human body to the natural flow of energy. It is the women who remind me that the body can connect directly with the moon, which in turn offers a connection with the ocean tides. It is this experience of connecting with the menstruation process, once removed, that sensitizes me to the center of the body's medicine wheel, the solar plexus. It also provides me with an experiential model for male/female relationships that have a maximum potential for teamwork and healthy interdependence. Such a view contrasts with the sexual wars of our day and the devastation of codependence.

CONCLUDING COMMENTS

The visionary selves, then, offer a wider vision of the selves. This wider vision moves the seeker from one plateau of growth to another. As the vision unfolds, the seeker notices significant tension, not only between the subpersonalities, but also within them. Avoiding the awareness of the energetic tensions between parts results in bonding patterns that snuff out intimacy in relationships. Developing awareness of the various parts and the dynamic tensions paves the way for using the energetics of these inner pulls as a fuel of the transforming process. It is to the inner tension between the subpersonalities that we now turn.

REFERENCE

Bateson, G. (1979). *Mind and nature: A necessary unity.* New York: Dutton.

6

Selves in Tension

Thus far we have looked at the growth/consciousness process of Bob and Betty and of Marv and a few of his clients as illustrative of our own evolutionary pilgrimage. We have looked at them from different angles, at both their individual journeys and the flavor of their bonding in relationship. Now, in this chapter, we delve deeper into the nature of the subpersonalities, into how these subflows of energy oppose each other or otherwise enter into tension, and into the dynamics of the transformational process through the voicing of these subpersonalities.

An ancient Lakota myth captures my attention in this regard. It is one of the two or three richest myths of Native America and appears most often under the title of "The White Buffalo Woman" (Black Elk, 1971). Years ago, when it was first told to me by my grandfather, it immediately registered in my consciousness as "The Many-Colored Buffalo," a title that just popped into my mind. When people truly experience a myth, it becomes their own as much as if they dreamed it, including the title. Your heading for this primordial story may differ both from the traditional one and from mine.

Earlier, we sampled this myth, and now we spend more time with its wisdom. Two Lakota hunters, close as brothers, were out on a hunting expedition with their bows and arrows. As they stood on a hill searching the horizon for game, they noticed something in the distance coming toward them. The more they gazed, the less their senses told them and the more mysterious the object appeared. At last, it was close enough that they could decipher that it was a woman dressed in white buckskin, bearing a bundle on her back. And not just *a* woman, it was a *beautiful* woman!

One of the hunters turned to the other and voiced his curiosity, as well as his mounting desire for her. The first was horrified and scolded his companion, telling him he should not have such thoughts and must not act on them. The two of them argued intensely over whether it was good or bad for him to harbor these desires and did not notice that the woman drew close to them, putting down her bundle.

Assessing their conflict, she invited the one who desired her to approach, which he did eagerly, licking his lips. As he joined the woman, they were covered by a great cloud. When it lifted, the mysterious woman was standing alone. At her feet was the skeleton of the man with a mass of snakes consuming his flesh.

"Behold what you see!" the strange woman said to the remaining hunter, who had lectured his mate. "Go tell your chief that I wish to tell you something of great importance."

Considerably impressed, the remaining hunter returned to the council. They declared him to be good and decreed that his hunting companion was bad. Time passed, and, at last, the woman arrived at the tribal council as she had promised. She took the bundle from her back and explained that it held the sacred pipe. With the pipe, she explained, they could *send their voices to Wakan Tanka, the Sacred Mystery.*

On the side of the red stone bowl of the pipe were seven circles in the shape of a spiral. Each of these, she continued, represented a cycle of life and a ceremonial rite during which the pipe was to be used. The circles also represented seven days, and, she further taught, the people would be alive as long as they *sent their voices to the Sacred Mystery on a daily basis.* She promised to return to help the people in the transition from one age to another.

Moving around the lodge in a sun-wise manner, the mysterious woman now walked away from them. After trundling a short distance, she looked back toward the people and sat down. As she sat there, a cloud, like the earlier one that concealed the snakes, settled over her. When she arose, the people were amazed to see that she had become a young red-and-brown buffalo calf, a newborn. The calf walked further, lay down, and rolled, looking back at the people, again stirring up a cloud of dust.

When she arose this time, she was a white buffalo. Again, she walked further and rolled on the ground, kicking up another cloud of dust. This time, though, they could see through the cloud as the change was taking place: they saw the white buffalo becoming a black buffalo. This buffalo then walked farther away from the people, stopped, bowed to each of the four quarters of the universe, and disappeared over the hill.

THE SPLIT IN THE PERSON

What first protrudes out of this remarkable myth is the story of the two hunters, reminiscent of the two brothers in the prodigal son, a parable from the teachings of Jesus. The story makes clear the early split in the individual between that part which is primitive and instinctual and the part that holds back the instinctual.

The story of the two hunters portrays all our stories; it is the account of the separation between our primary selves and our disowned selves. It is the account of how one set of energy patterns is at home outdoors and another is at home indoors, how one is passionate and the other impersonal, and how one is irrational and the other rational.

In the face of the stress of the approaching woman and awakening desire, the myth tells us that the natural course is for this inner struggle to reach a conclusion. And what is the outcome?

The flesh is eaten off the instinctual self by snakes, a repugnant image indeed! It appears that this energy has permanently disappeared and that "good" has triumphed. This impression gains more weight when the remaining hunter returns to the tribal council. The council pronounces that the remaining hunter is good, and the vanquished hunter is bad. Yet we are surprised later in the myth when we discover that the instinctual energy returns in the form of a buffalo changing its colors.

The myth clearly tells us that every primary self within the person has another energy unit in dynamic tension with it. Every primary self with which we identify, because we deem it to be good, has one or more disowned units of energy of equal and usually opposite energy. Sometimes the poles are oppositional and sometimes in tension in other ways. In this way the myth is a secret map of forbidding and unknown inner territory of every person. When the myth reaches the point of the woman changing into the many colored buffalo, it comments on the direction of the transformation process. Before we delve deeper into that portion of the myth, we need to spend more time with the tension between the selves.

Recall the account of Bob and Betty for a moment. A primary self that Bob presented to the outside world was that of a competent, well-intentioned, pleasing man. As a CPA, he made an excellent living by using these primary selves. When his wife started having affairs and developed alcoholism, a range of polarized selves broke through, ones that had nothing to do with his CPA practice. These selves were jealous, enraged, and quite dangerous to him, since they had been split off at an early age, just as the myth describes.

After a few months in the course of therapy, Bob puzzled over this dream: "The electricity is cut off in my office on a Friday afternoon. My secretary, who in the dream looks more conservative than usual, has moved to answer my office telephone in front of the house of a sexy girl I grew up with, one I dated when I was in junior high school. She was one of the sexiest people I've ever known.

"She also had a questionable reputation. When I arrive at my office, two black guys in a Porsche are parked in front. Maybe they are drug dealers, I think. I fly up by flapping my arms to take a look at them. Later, they're playing volleyball at my old junior high school. I join them and jump up to the ceiling and touch my belly button. They are impressed. Later, we play basketball, and I tell them I can shoot better than Michael Jordan. One of them offers to be my agent."

The opposites in this dream jump out, having been split off at some early phase of life. There is the CPA who works hard at his office; only, the electrical charge has gone out of that part of himself for the time being. It is a Friday afternoon: time to allow some other kind of energy out. His secretary moves, and where is it she moves? In front of the house of a sexy young woman from his junior high days. The picture of his reserved secretary and the sexy young woman forecast the opposites next to be revealed in the dream.

Now the stage is set for an opposite and disowned self to dance out onto the stage of his consciousness. This opposite or disowned self is symbolized in the dream by the two black guys in the fast automobile who may well be drug dealers. Bob's challenge is to separate from the primary self, the CPA, enough to acknowledge the subself that likes fast cars, maybe drugs.

First, he must gain the permission of the primary selves, symbolized by the CPA, who make the rules up for how he runs his life. Then, he can talk directly to the owners of the Porsche. That he is ready to have this conversation is symbolized in the dream by the part of him who can lift off the ground enough to gain a view of the two black men. This symbol in the dream speaks of a beginning aware ego, the executive self who can stand between two poles without being overly attached to either.

As he talks to the drug dealer, he discovers a part of himself that actually would like to abuse drugs, a part of himself that buys Betty beer even when she is struggling with acknowledging her alcoholism. Rather than face the opposite in himself, he has married a person who is opposite in this one aspect, maybe in others as well. In this way, the instinctual part that he left for dead in a pile of snakes comes back at him from both his dreams and his relationships.

WOUNDS OF THE DISOWNED SELVES

Why are these disowned selves, in tension with the primary selves, often nasty when they return to the scene? The myth depicts them as a mass of snakes in their disowned state, not exactly an image of a happy camper.

Does the myth tell us that the first hunter is "bad" because of his curiosity and sexual desire? No! It points out that he sustains a wound in the conflict so that only his skeleton remains and the tribal council labels him as being "bad." This statement of the myth doesn't mean that the myth condemns sexuality or even selfishness, as some interpreters contend. Rather, it merely points to the inevitable process of the split where one part gets labeled "good" and the other "bad."

Somewhere in the process the wounds occur, some deeper than others, but none of us escape these wounds of childhood. The wounding process continues throughout life in such a way that old wounds are continually picked at as the scabs become infected. We will explore these wounds more thoroughly in the next chapter.

THE THANKLESS TASK OF THE PRIMARY SELVES

The "good guy" returns to the tribe to tell his story and receive the decree that he is indeed good. After we split off from the more primitive aspects of ourselves, the good guys take over in an attempt at self-parenting. By the good guys I refer to the primary selves so familiar to most of us: the inner critic, the perfectionist, the judge, and the pleaser, to acknowledge some of the more popular survivor selves.

Once in power they drive the primitive selves deeper underground. For example, the television evangelist, Jimmy Swaggart, once told of a dream he had over twenty years ago where he met "the devil" in the form of a reptile. He fought with this devil until he finally overcame the devil, killed it. To his audience, he declared that he awakened feeling grateful that the battle with Satan was victorious. The dragon, he declared joyously, was slain.

To those of us who fight the battle and feel the tension between the good guys (primary selves) and bad guys (disowned selves), the dream sounds familiar. It is, in fact, an archetypal dream, one common to most humans at one time or another. But the conflict was not over. The primitive only went underground for twenty years. When it appeared again, was it ever unruly, angry, and determined to be heard!

His instinctual self in its disowned form, according to my view, erupted in the behavior of his visiting prostitutes in motels. He so split the instinctual self off that the primary selves believed the other didn't exist. This time the battle aired, not in his dreams, but on national television.

The "I told you so" energy that appeared in me when I first heard of this dream only pointed to the continuing sweating I do between similar opposites—the part of me that wants freedom to do what I want when I want with whomever I want, and the part of me that wants the safety of loyalty and integrity.

So, the primary selves (the good guys) do the best they can to keep the car on the road, and they honestly believe that we must do away with the primitive selves. They learned what to disown by looking at what was unacceptable to our families of origin. Sometimes, the families would have an active war against certain primitive energies. Some families, for example, drive the segments of the person that desire human touch underground; they accomplish this task simply by refusing to touch the child. In other instances, the repression is accomplished simply through the grimace of a mouth or the raising of an eyebrow.

These primary selves soon learn how to do the repressing themselves; they are well trained. They succeed in the sense that they buy us time in a world that does not honor the primitive, and they get very little acknowledgement from us, or from psychotherapists and other teachers, for their efforts. The fact of the matter is that many psychotherapists are in open warfare against the primary selves. They want to do away with these more conservative elements of the personality and thus free the person. Conferences on "resistant" clients are thinly veiled attacks on the primary selves. Nothing could be further from the truth in this approach that I describe here.

THE SWEAT BETWEEN OPPOSITES

The easy way out for the primary selves is to eliminate the opposites, as described in the myth and in Jimmy Swaggart's dream. When the transformational process heats up, awareness comes to the executive self so that it can see the primary parts and know them. These parts are "smoked out," as the pipe symbolizes, and then the unconscious begins to send up images of the opposites to the stage of the conscious mind through dreams, memories, fantasies, visions, prayers, and meditations.

As they are "smoked out," the aware ego is born to sit between the two opposites and listen to the dialogue between the two. Most of us live life without this kind of awareness. It is surprising how easily it comes into being once we wake up from the long sleep of allowing our primary selves to run our lives, and learn how to facilitate listening to these voices.

Listening to the voices of the opposites through the aware ego adds a dynamic quality to life, as Bob found out. Return for a moment to his dream. On the one hand, he was a CPA. On the other hand, he had these disowned selves that like to drive fast cars, handle drugs, and participate in sexual extravaganzas, at least in his dreams. When these images first came to the surface, and when he entered an aware state where he could entertain both at the same time in his mind, he started to sweat.

I mean literally sweat; it poured off him.

How could both the organizing energy of the CPA and the flashy energy of the fast cars and sexy drives co-exist? The sweat increased for weeks as he felt pulled first one way and then another, but at last he sensed how he could use both of these energies. Boy, was his wife, Betty, overjoyed. She loved this new flashy energy and stated for the first time she was glad that she had given up her affair.

THE SWEAT IN BONDING PATTERNS

This teasing or smoking out of the opposite parts helps in the breaking of useless bonding patterns that rule most relationships. My wife, Judith, and I once spent several days in the home of friends, in lively development of awareness of these various parts. I thought I was really on top of things. After dark one evening, we drove on a rural road in the fog near the Northern California coast, digesting the rich interactions we had with the delightful couple we were visiting. A truck listed over into our lane so that I had to swerve slightly; the heat in the car (or was it in me?) caused sweat to pop out on my forehead.

Under this stress, a covey of primary survivor selves came to the fore to take over without my being aware of them. "We need to do something about this damned heat," the angry father in me declared harshly.

Judith's helpful but scared little girl was called forth by this harsh energy in me. "I'll see what I can do," she replied in a pert but tight voice.

Then, she laughed: "We just bonded."

I angrily denied it and squeezed the steering wheel tightly while I sent more harsh energy her way. I don't know what she was doing, but she wasn't buying into this bonding pattern. With no partner to enter that familiar bonding pattern, a moment of awareness settled over me. I saw that I was speaking in a harsh, critical father voice.

Where, I asked myself, was its disowned opposite?

The sweat increased as I searched and soon found a scared little boy who didn't want to drive in the fog. He had wanted some help, and so the harsh and critical father, in this moment of stress, leapt to his rescue. Now the sweat really increased as I sat in awareness between these two opposites—the scared little boy and the powerful but critical father energies inside.

Who would I channel next to the outside world and how? "Don't admit you're wrong," screamed the heavy duty primary self. "Tell her about me," the other, scared one whispered.

It seemed like hours, but was only a few minutes before I said to Judith, "I think I've located a scared part of myself. This fog really scares me."

"It scared me, too," she said softly. "I'll help you watch and give you a back rub when we get to Hal and Sidra's."

So go the tiny moments of transformation. Not that this breath of awareness meant that we would not bond this way again. We would, of course; it's part of our human condition. Yet these moments of awareness come more quickly and last longer.

I've worked long and hard to separate out this harsh father who comes out mainly with those I love. It has been even more tedious to smoke out the scared parts who are alert to the slightest moment of danger. At first, I tried to ignore the frightened little boy and thus to disown him. Later, when I separated out the harsh father, I tried to send him to prison. But he came out speaking the language of whatever psychology or theology I happened to be into at the time. Both are slowly changing as I learn to enter the sweat of sitting between them.

THE STAGES OF TRANSFORMATION

Next, the myth points to the stages of transformation. On the side of the bowl of the redstone pipe are seven circles that form a spiral. Each of these circles represent a major transition both in the individual and in the evolution of the planet. The Buffalo Woman promises to be present at each of these major transitions.

Each major developmental phase of the individual in relationship offers an opportunity for increased transformation of consciousness. These pregnant moments (called *kairos* by the Greeks) are particularly evident at moments of learning to walk, of leaving home, of middle-age "crazes," of retiring, and of facing death, to name just a few. During these *kairos* moments of crisis, the heat of our life situations is turned up, and we have an opportunity to sweat. With the sweat comes the opportunity of new awareness.

What happens with many of us is that we weather the heat like a fever, and, in fact, we tend to call it a sickness. Some of us manage to get medicated for it, since at those times we may feel depressed. The cause for the depression may well be that the disowned selves are near the surface, and that we spend much energy through our primary selves keeping them down.

Some, though, use the heat of the crisis to make a commitment to themselves, and an invisible line is crossed—the line of surrendering to the process of evolution and transformation. For example, Betty first just wanted to get over her alcoholism. Through Alcoholics Anonymous she discovered that she would have to acknowledge the voices that craved alcohol the rest of her life. There were no shortcuts.

From this realization she began to think about the lifelong process of personal growth and evolution, but she was not committed to it yet. One day, after two years in AA and in group therapy, she came in mad as a hornet. The group helped her access the part of her that was angry; it spoke: "I'm mad at you, Taegel, because I've been coming here for nearly two years, and I'm not well yet. I still get in these terrible fights with Bob, and I still want to drink nearly every day. So fuck you, and fuck this group—and fuck the Higher Power, while you're at it."

Something about surfacing this energy stimulated her aware ego, and a few weeks later she spoke from a more aware executive self: "I've been thinking. So what if I have to struggle with alcohol the rest of my life? Look at all I've learned about myself as a result of that travail. Maybe Bob and I will make it, and maybe we won't. But the main thing here is I'm learning so much about myself from our bonding patterns. I'm going to do what it takes to keep knowing these things that pop out of my dreams. I'm going to get out of this group before too long, but I'm in this growth thing for the duration."

Transformation comes, then, in an unfolding rhythm. Now we are ready to sense this rhythm.

RETURN OF THE PRIMITIVE

In the myth of Buffalo Woman, it appears in the beginning that we have just another moralistic story telling us that it is wrong to feel sexual. If a person allows too much passion, according to this interpretation, the consequences are dire—being eaten by snakes. But at the end of the story, the tribal members are immensely surprised that this beautiful woman turns into an animal, a return to the primitive.

Instead of escaping from the animal within, the myth tells us to embrace the animal. Through the embracing we will be transformed. The myth thus discloses the rhythm of transformation: the split of good and bad, the facing of the many in the lodge, and the return to the instinctual.

It is quite interesting that many accounts of this myth will omit this conclusion of where the holy woman turns back into a buffalo which continues to transform into other buffaloes and other colors. This omission occurs because it is so easy to view the myth as a story of passionate brother gone bad and a prudent brother who prevails. When the primitive energy returns in the form of the buffalo who takes precedence over the human manifestation, it is no longer a simple moralistic tale. It is an encouragement to embrace the primitive without being overpowered, as was the passionate brother. The return of the primitive in dreams and fantasies often can signal that the seeker is at the edge of making a quantum leap on the transforming spiral.

Marv brought in a series of dreams about horses told to him by one of his clients, Kay I'll call her. Kay was a very bright woman in her late thirties who had immense talent but who, because she was the continuing "baby" of the family of origin, did not claim her power. She thought of herself as being sickly and unable to say "no." Her family was quite repressed, except when her parents got out of control with their alcoholism. One of the early dreams saw her riding a black-and-white horse by the name of "Killer." In another she rode a horse with a large rump who didn't like saddles or bridles; he preferred that she ride bareback and guide him by using his mane.

In one dream she looked at different kinds of water and found herself in a car, sitting in the back seat while a man drove out into the water in order to kill himself. He decided against it and drove to shore. She got out and told him that she would not drive with him any more. In the last dream of this series, she was on a large work horse, a Clydesdale type, which was so big that it could wade across the ominous river she had been observing and into which the suicidal man had driven her. She was not yet on the horse, but she was glad that it was big enough and strong enough to take her across when she needed to go.

Marv was excited that she had had this series of dreams, because he interpreted them to mean that she was contacting the primitive side of herself symbolized by the horses. He further explained that she had been on a walk in the country and that a large brown horse had come up to her and nuzzled her. On that same walk, she had found a horseshoe and used it as a symbol of her current emerging into a more powerful and assertive woman.

She had also told how, the week after these dreams, she had become openly angry with a college friend who was visiting her from out of state. This anger had enabled her to keep a boundary that had been violated by this friend for years.

In the supervising process we pointed out to Marv, not only that was she making contact with the horse within, but also that the primitive symbol of the horse was showing up in her life through her walks. We suggested to him that he could think of the horse that nuzzled her as his co-worker in Kay's transforming process. This suggestion puzzled him at the time, but he would become more familar with what it meant as he moved along the path himself. The animal as ally in transformation will be further discussed in the remaining chapters.

To return to the myth—first, the woman turns into a buffalo calf, calling attention to the child within all of us. Acknowledging these little children within launches transformation. Second, she changes into a white buffalo. The white buffalo represents the importance of awareness and, in my way of thinking, is the aware ego, the chief self. Once awareness channels into the ego, there is a function in the person to receive the voices of the different parts. It is the aware ego who tunes into these various voices and gains more choices. I believe the white buffalo is held sacred because, as awareness expands, it leads to an underlying and universal energy, a being energy that will be explored in the chapter on spiritual selves.

Third, she does not stop at this point of transformation. Already the tribe has called one hunter good and another bad, so she wants to leave them something to chew on for a few thousand years. She transforms into a black buffalo, symbol of darkness. This transformation adds even a richer texture to the story because it is the black buffalo, not the white one, who performs the sacred act of bowing to the four directions of the Sacred Spirit. To me, the meaning is clear: Through awareness of the deeper instincts lies the pathway to God.

It is in the form of the black buffalo that she disappears over the horizon. This portion of the story dramatically tells of the importance of the shadow selves, those instinctual selves that have become split off from us because they were not acceptable to various members of our families of origin or the culture in which we grew. When voiced and visioned, the very selves that we threw to the snakes become the leaders in the multicolored pathway of transformation.

REFERENCE

Black Elk. (1971). *The sacred pipe: Black Elk's account of the seven rites of the Oglala Sioux* (J. Brown, Ed.). New York: Penguin Books.

7

The Hidden Selves

In the last chapter we looked at some of the bipolar energies pulling in tension against each other and suggested that often one of the energies exists in a state largely hidden from the conscious mind. In this chapter the focus becomes even sharper on the hidden selves that have experienced various wounds. That these wounded selves are hidden blocks their healing.

The myth of the White Buffalo Woman—the Many Colored Buffalo, as I prefer to call it—continues to shed light on these selves, but an additional lens is required to discern the often obscure nature of these hidden selves. Since they are hidden, they are not easily experienced. Jung (1977) explores the relationship between the ego and the unconscious and makes the humorous point that the unconscious is difficult to discern precisely because it is unconscious. With this guideline in mind, we turn to a myth of the Painted Arrow People (Storm, 1972) that provides the necessary light to look in the shadows of the unconscious and preconscious for these hidden and wounded selves.

Once there was a mouse. A busy mouse he was, who spent all day every day searching for food and surviving. One day, though, he noticed that there was a roar in the background and asked several of his mouse colleagues about it. They busied themselves with finding food and ignored him.

Later, in his tedium, he bumped into a large, furry creature. Scared, he started to run, but heard a voice: "It is I, your brother raccoon."

They talked for a while, and the mouse told his new friend about the roar. The raccoon explained that the roar was a river, and he offered to show him the hidden body of water.

Now the mouse was in a quandary: his brother mice had told him he couldn't survive if he spent his time in idle curiosity finding out what the roar was. Because of this he was tempted to turn down the raccoon's invitation. At last, though, he chose to follow his curiosity and adventure. The little mouse, his tiny heart pounding in his breast, followed his new friend until at last they came to the river.

It was huge and breathtaking, deep and clear in some places, murky in others. Its force and majesty overpowered little mouse. Just as he was taking all these sights in, the raccoon introduced him to another friend, the green frog. After a brief talk, the raccoon explained that he must fish the river and left little mouse with his new guide. When little mouse approached the river, he looked at his reflection and saw a frightened mouse. He then asked the frog if he was afraid, but the frog explained that he had been in and around the river since birth and that he felt at home there.

To help the little mouse, the frog offered to introduce him to medicine power. He proposed to do this by teaching him to jump, explaining that it would help with fear. After much instruction little mouse jumped as high as he could, but fell into the water.

Boy, was he angry!

He felt he had been tricked, but then the frog asked him what he had seen when he was at the top of his jump.

"A majestic mountain," he replied.

From that day on the little mouse had a new name: He was now known everywhere as "Jumping Mouse." He then returned to his people and told them of his many experiences and of his vision of the mountain, but they did not believe him. They thought him daft. They argued vigorously with him that he should not spend his time with such fantasies, because he should be hunting for food and preparing for winter.

Time passed.

He could not forget his vision, so, despite the warnings of his fellow mice, he prepared for another leg of the journey. He went past the river this time to the edge of the known world, a place called the prairie. High above he could see a sky filled with spots, all eagles that fed on mice, whether they could jump or not. True, he was afraid, but he also listened to the sound of his courage and ran out onto the rolling plains.

After a long travel, he stopped under a sage bush and met an old mouse who told him the history of the prairie, with special attention to the dangers. He offered Jumping Mouse a secure place with much food and advised him to forget his vision of the mountain, telling him it was only a rumor.

Yet Jumping Mouse felt he must continue to follow his vision. Out on the prairie again, he trudged along, wary of every step. As he stopped to rest, he heard heavy breathing. Investigating, he saw a prodigious mound of hair with black horns, a great buffalo, lying down.

Jumping Mouse asked him why he lay on the ground and found that the huge beast was sick and dying and that only the eye of a mouse could heal him. Since the buffalo had never seen a mouse, he didn't believe they existed.

After much inner debate, Jumping Mouse told the sick buffalo that he was a mouse and that he would donate one of his two eyes. As soon as he uttered these words, one of his eyes flew out of his head and the buffalo was healed.

With that the buffalo offered to allow Jumping Mouse to walk under him so the eagles would not spot him. The buffalo also knew the way to the mountain and offered his services as a guide. The journey now was in some ways safer but in other ways still dangerous. Jumping Mouse only had one eye, and he had constantly to avoid the hooves of the large buffalo. The beast helped him and yet at any moment could destroy him.

At last, they reached the foot of the mountain, where the buffalo left him. Now, in this new place, he soon ran into another large creature, a wolf. Once again, he could see that the wolf was ill, so ill in fact that he couldn't lift his head. Jumping mouse recognized the wolf as his long-standing enemy, but he now knew that his eyes could heal. After another long debate, he offered his one remaining eye to the wolf. Once again, his eye immediately flew out and entered the wolf. The wolf was made whole.

Grateful, the wolf offered his services as a guide to take him up the mountain to the great medicine lake. This leg of the journey went slow and was the most dangerous because Jumping Mouse walked in high places with no eyes. He had to depend entirely on a being who had been a long-standing enemy. At last, they arrived at the shore of the great medicine lake, and the wolf had to leave him so he could guide others.

Jumping Mouse sat there trembling in fear. It was no use running, for he was blind. But he knew this lake was the home of the eagles and that one would soon find him and eat him. Presently, he felt a shadow on his back and heard the heart-thumping eagle cry. He braced himself for the shock, and the eagle hit.

Jumping Mouse went to sleep.

Then, he awakened.

Was he ever surprised to be alive. Now, he could see. Everything was blurry, but the colors were beautiful. A faintly familiar figure approached and asked him if he wanted new medicine. This agreed, Jumping Mouse was invited to crouch down and jump as high as he could and to hang onto the wind and trust.

Jump he did: he closed his eyes and hung onto the wind, and it carried him higher and higher. He opened his eyes, and they were clear. Even from this high altitude he could see his old friend upon a lily pad on the great medicine lake. It was the frog.

"You have a new name," called the frog up to him, "You are Eagle."

A PROGRESSION OF HIDDEN SUBPERSONALITIES

This myth offers another fascinating map of the inner topography of human beings and their relationships with other living creatures. As we follow, it leads and introduces us to a progression of hidden selves that lead eventually to our inner wounds. First comes the raccoon, then the frog, then the mountain, then the river, then the older mouse, then the buffalo, then the wolf, then the medicine lake, and finally the eagle. This progression leads away from the familiar primary selves, symbolized by the mouse community, to the partially seen selves that are not so frightening, and therefore only partially disowned, symbolized by the raccoon and the frog.

As seekers listen to the various voices and behold the new visions, the hidden selves come forward in a progression that takes them deeper and deeper into the psyche and introduce them to wounded selves that have been long disowned, such as those symbolized by the buffalo, the wolf, the medicine lake, and finally the eagle.

Put another way, the unfolding of transformation moves from knowing the primary (or survival) selves to experiencing the less developed but somewhat known selves, and finally to the hidden and more frightening selves, frightening because they carry pain.

After he speaks of his discontent with the progression of his growth, Bob has a dream that both clarifies his position and charts a number of hidden energies for him to explore as a way to continue the transforming journey. This dream, though different in content from the dream cited in the previous chapter, has a similar progression of hidden subselves that are seeking to be known by the aware ego.

The dream: "I'm on a bus bound for Austin. A rumor spreads on the bus that one of th passengers, a punk rocker, may have killed himself. His brother has also killed himself, and I see him fall off the top of the bus. Strangely, he is not dead or even badly hurt.

"Later, I see a guide who turns into a chicken with an eagle's beak and bites my hand, but I am strong enough to resist the bite. It hurts only a little.

"Then the guide and his friend shoot up with drugs, and I feel disgust that they are not any more advanced than that. I feel the power of a jungle cat coming on me, sorta like a man changes into a werewolf. I crouch down and roar. At first, I am terrified of this jungle cat, but then I feel somehow safer that this jungle cat in me will help me should I feel like taking drugs."

The progression of hidden selves jumped out of the dream for Bob. First, the punk rocker was somewhat familiar to Bob because he had come to like this kind of music, a departure from his CPA mode. Then, there was the punk rocker's brother who tried to commit suicide, and Bob would discover in the weeks that followed, in talking to this aspect, that the potential of destruction in his family and marriage exists in the rocker. When he went to dances, he felt like having sex, and not only with his wife. Plus, it was in dancing to this music that his wife originally met the man with whom she had an affair. Bob was coming to love the part of him that moves to this music. Yet there was danger.

Then it turned out, in the dream, that a guide on the transformational journey was into drugs. As Bob talked to this dream segment, he discovered a guide, a subpersonality, that was at first terrifying to him. The guide had many important bits of wisdom for him, but finally wanted Bob to take drugs to help him face certain feelings. If he was bored, anxious, depressed, or angry, the energy suggested drugs.

Bob became even more aware of how he had spun this energy in himself out toward his wife Betty. For years, he had criticized her for trying to solve her problems with alcohol and other prescribed drugs. He had no patience with her, yet here in his dream he faced this aspect of himself. Had he through the years projected the alcoholic tendencies in himself out onto his wife? The dream confirmed this shocking probability—shocking, at least, to him.

In the dream in the previous chapter, he began a conversation with the drivers of the Porsche whom he suspected of taking drugs. Now that aspect of himself became even clearer. On his agenda was getting to know this part of him that was potentially drug dependent; also, the drug voice must be allowed to speak. If not, it would lurk in the background, seeking out and drawing drug-dependent people into Bob's life so the drug energy could speak to him through them. Until he could face the subselves that carried his own pain, he would continue to draw other people's pain toward him.

At the bottom of this particular progression of hidden selves was the jungle cat. Just as in the dream, Bob was at first terrified of the cat and its naked power. However, as he evolved in his awareness of the cat inside him, he slowly but surely trusted that power.

This dream occurred after Bob began his conversations with the catalpa tree in his backyard. As he had sat in his backyard the night of the dream, he had the urge to pitch a tent and sleep out as he had when he was a child. After the dream, this urge continued until one day he lay in the sun with one of his children. As he lay there, his stomach throbbing in connection with the earth, the image of the jungle cat came powerfully back to him.

He was surprised in the months that followed that he could call on this jungle energy to help him in his various compulsions with food and alcohol. As he learned to experience the inner jungle cat, he learned that this cat would eat and drink only what he needed. Jungle cats generally don't overeat or overdrink, he came to realize. When he felt the impulse to overeat, he just called on the cat. The more the cat possessed him, the less he felt the compulsive energy. Key here is not the intellectual realization that he had a jungle cat inside but rather the continuing *experience* of that cat.

Recall a basic assumption of this approach to transformation is that consciousness consists of awareness *plus the experience of an aspect. Then, the experience of a specific energy is brought back through awareness to the ego.*

Both the dream and the myth strongly suggest that each of us has a number of progressions of subpersonalities, moving from the more familiar (with which we overidentify) to the less familiar (which we disown.) *This flow is an energetic continuum that moves in a spiral, from defending energy through vulnerable energy into the abyss where are found the primitive energies that respond to rocks, trees, and other creatures. These instinctual energies from the abyss assist with those inner aspects that have been deeply wounded.*

THE BRIDGE BETWEEN THE AWARE EGO AND THE HIDDEN SELVES

The raccoon provides a bridge between usual consciousness and hidden consciousness: The mouse meets him as a departure from his usual reality, yet is not terribly frightening.

Raccoons are like that; they come into campgrounds at night to browse for food. Rarely are they seen in the daytime, mostly at night. While not as familiar as a dog or a cat, they are still a gentle introduction to the forest and the wilds. Our usual power selves are more at home with domesticated animals, especially dogs. Of the domesticated animals, cats generally make our primary selves most "itchy," because cats maintain a strong element of wildness despite their domestication. This dimension of wildness in common cats may explain why more people tend to be allergic to cats than to dogs, since we as a culture seem allergic to our own wildness. Out a bit further on this progression of wild energy lies the raccoon.

In the dream cited earlier in this chapter, the bridge is the image (subpersonality) of sitting on an ordinary bus, hearing the rumor of a suicidal punk rocker. This image carries a little charge, yet is not so bold as to turn Bob off. The rumor of an experience is not nearly so threatening as the first-hand experience.

Whether it is through exploring a dream or some other access, the unconscious will provide a bridge from our usual awareness to the world of the hidden. It is important to find the bridge patiently through the hunter selves without jumping too quickly into the sensational feelings of the dramatic and wounded selves.

If the seeker jumps too quickly through an enthusiastic facilitator into the more spectacular hidden selves, the survival selves will object loudly through a backlash. They will object so loudly that they will bring the exploration to a momentary halt.

As can be seen in the myth, the primary (survival) selves are quite conservative and do not like these sudden bursts of awareness. When we first awaken in the morning (before the primary selves are fully awake and on the job), the dreams are more easily accessible, yet they are not there in their entirety. These moments provide bridges between the world of the known and unknown selves. Later in the day the primary selves block this awareness in the interest of survival tasks.

Another importance of finding a bridge between the aware ego and the hidden selves is that many units of energy are disowned only for a particular bonding pattern or transaction. For instance, Bob could own his interest in rock music fairly easily even though it didn't fit with his basic CPA image, so the subpersonality that loved rock music was recovered in the deeper sense. The conservative part of him that disliked the music and felt judgmental faded farther into the background.

When he had one of his clients with him in his car, he found himself animatedly tapping the dash board to the rollicking rock sound of Prince. With a critical tone in his voice, his client asked him if he actually liked that silly music. Immediately, Bob defended the whole world of rock music and attacked his client for his uptight narrow-mindedness. In response the client muttered something about how Bob had changed and that, once, Bob had told him how disgusting rock music was. For the moment of that bonding pattern Bob had disowned a former primary self, the critic of rock music.

INTRODUCTION TO THE UGLY

Next on the progression of hidden selves is the frog, generic representative of the ugly in literature and dreamlife. On the road of transformation the inner frog inevitably comes up, an energy that at first startles the seeker.

Early in the process Betty spoke of a horrifying daydream she had about one of her daughters. In the daydream her daughter died in an auto accident, and, to her great horror, Betty was relieved, even glad, that it had happened. She was horrified at the ugliness of this daydream, and it was with considerable shame that she brought it out into the open. The daydream showed her froglike energy hiding in her psyche.

On closer look, however, she listened to what the gladness over death in the dream meant. It meant that she could be free for a moment of the awesome responsibility of being the parent of a teenager.

Since she had little opportunity to rebel as a teenager, this part of her told her that she was angry at her daughter for going through a rebellious stage she had never experienced until she had an affair. The voice of the "frog" also told her that she resented her daughter's budding sexuality as well as her youth and vitality. As soon as she could look at the energy in the light of awareness, she immediately felt the other balancing energy of the love of the inner mother.

There never was any question about her truly wanting her daughter dead as an executive decision; however, Betty came to understand that one small part of her thought of that, ugly though it first seemed. Yet, the very shock of this ugliness became a teacher that in turn introduced her to her inner rebel. Through this daydream she began to see that her affair was not about love but rather about many other aspects of herself, including the rebel.

Another example: Marv brought a case to supervision that included a "redneck" who was abusing his wife and children. Marv felt an overpowering urge to stand up and lecture his client, and sometimes he felt like hitting the man. The muscles in his jaws bulged as he talked about the reprehensible behavior of this man who had come to him for therapy. He was particularly revulsed by an account where his client had essentially raped his wife when she had awakened in the night to find her husband inside her. She protested but he would not relent.

Members of Marv's training group asked him if he had ever felt like abusing a woman. At first he protested that he absolutely had not, but then an energy flicked across his face. I inquired if his protective selves would allow this energy to come out in the open so that Marv could know it better. With some hesitancy his ruling energy allowed the interview to occur.

Once out in the open this energetic subpart identified itself as "Bubba." Bubba was an aspect of Marv that he had long suppressed; it liked to drink beer, get into brawls, and chase women. It is not surprising that Marv would have such an aspect, since he grew up in a blue-collar neighborhood. His childhood role models of male behavior were filled with a variety of Bubbas. Yet, as he had become a sophisticated psychotherapist, he had pushed this energy so far down that it had no voice whatsoever. It was ugly to Marv, so it was banished to the hinterlands of his personality.

As is often the case, Nature sent Marv a client who embodied in the extremity the energy that he had disowned. As soon as he owned this energy, Marv did not have to spend much time figuring out what to do with the client. He, in fact, already knew how to work with this client; it was this "ugly" energy within that was blocking the work that he knew how to do. Now, with it out in the open, he was free to choose a creative path rather than lecture his client, which had really been a lecture to himself to keep Bubba under control.

This example surfaces a knotty issue in the psychotherapy process: what to do with the interior "Bubbas" and their kin who reside in psychotherapists. Traditional psychotherapy has put this energy under the heading of countertransference and assumed the therapist would seek out therapy on his or her own. Often therapists do not seek out therapy, and when they do, they often do not find therapists who are equipped to access these ugly energies.

Thus, the therapy bogs down in a discussion about these more basic energies, but the experience of the energies usually does not happen. The subpersonalities that conduct the psychotherapy are those that want to reason and gain rational insight; they want to lecture or label the Bubbas of the world. Write it down: The Bubbas of the world do not respond to reason or lecturing or even insight gained through analysis.

In our training program we work with the hypothesis that no male therapist can work with an abusive male until he has faced the inner abuser, felt the darkness of its soul, and sensed its overwhelming urge to hit as a solution.

A corollary of that hypothesis is that almost all males in our society have an energy to rape inside somewhere, and that the best approach is to ferret that energy out. It will usually be a primitive energy that has gone sour, as we shall see. Similarly, we hypothesize that women therapists can effectively work with couples where abuse occurs only when they have ready access to a powerful and inner warrior, one that is not afraid to take on the abusive energy in the male.

BACK TO MOUSE CITY AND THE PROTECTOR SELVES

After Jumping Mouse leaves the river, he journeys, not onward to the sacred mountain, but backward to Mouse City. What does this mean? As the voicing with the hidden selves unfolds, it is necessary to return time and again to the primary or survival selves. They are suspicious of the new awareness that comes from these hidden selves. They are the inner conservatives that want us to slow down because they sense the danger that is to come.

What is the danger?

It is the pain of the wounded selves that we shall meet if we journey very far in this inner world. In order to help us survive, they have convinced us that we had happy childhoods where we were not severely hurt. They convinced us of this illusion in order for us to launch our lives. It was a necessary illusion. But now it is time to give up the illusion. No one escapes childhood without deep and excruciating pain.

These inner conservatives will tell us that the cost of time, energy, and money is too great and that we should not go on with this exploration. In the emerging aware ego, one can evaluate this information from the primary selves. Sometimes it fits to stay a while with them and conserve what one has learned. Finally, if the transformational journey is to continue, the call of the risking selves must be heeded. But the way back to Mouse City and the conservative protectors must not be forgotten or denied, for they are crucial.

THE FIRST LAYER OF WOUNDED SELVES

Next, Jumping Mouse meets the great buffalo who is sick and dying and can only be healed by the eye of a mouse. Significantly, Jumping Mouse first feels of the large mound of fur, not knowing what it is. Only as he talks to this mound of fur does he discover that it is a buffalo and that it is sick and dying.

So, along the way of the progression of hidden selves we meet those large aspects of the person that need to be talked to so they can tell us what is wrong with them. They hurt; they are wounded; they are dying within; they need something from us. This something they need is crucial to us and involves great sacrifice.

This early layer of wounded selves reveals the global nature of pain in our families of origin; hence the large buffalo. The recognition that the family itself is sick and dying, as far as deeper emotional nourishment is concerned, is painful. Few, if any, families escape periods of dysfunction, and where there is dysfunction there is painful abuse and neglect of the children—the actual children and the inner children of the adults.

The family of origin trip, especially at holiday time, offers the seeker clear access to the inner wounds of childhood, for, often, the patterns that produced the wounds are still there. Bob had long denied any problem with his family of origin, but as his awareness developed he began to observe patterns in his family that left him in an emotional toxic dump.

On a Mother's Day visit he took with him for the first time an aware ego, that ability within to stand at a distance and observe and then make more aware choices. He saw his mother treating his children with the same entrapping indulgence that she had used with him. He saw his father as a workaholic who had no time for his grandchildren. When he was with them, he was uncomfortable.

He noticed that his mother and father had no sense of play with each other, that his mother went elsewhere for emotional interaction, and that his father's only play seemed to be having a cocktail. He noticed how a principal pastime was speaking critically of other people.

These observances connected him with the little boy who had painfully recorded all these family patterns throughout childhood. They were so painful that he had developed a coping self that called all of the above "normal." At Christmas they visited Betty's parents each year, and now, through the aware ego, began to see similar patterns, only the use of chemicals was much greater.

Through participating in therapy groups and various training events, Bob and Betty listened to a variety of ways the inner children were wounded. Previously, they thought "wounds" meant severe physical battering of children. In these learning processes they were introduced to a variety of inner children who dwelled either inside of them or inside the other group participants, some of whom were terribly abused sexually. Some were beaten by baby sitters hired by parents who never knew. Others were physically and/or emotionally hurt by relatives, friends, housekeepers, yardworkers and teachers.

The terror of families broken by divorce or by death hit particularly hard on the little children inside who had been taken away from the safety they so desperately needed for their own development. Single parents doing the best they can still have to leave little children in precarious situations day after day.

Others suffered deep wounds from events they had never before considered, like intrusive enemas and overstimulation through showers and washings in the genital areas. Some were left alone with older siblings and cruelly beaten or otherwise abused. Since this was the only situation they had ever known, they just thought of it as normal. Common was the pain and confusion that came from sexual contact with a sibling where the parents did not provide safe boundaries.

Some discovered little children who had not been physically abused but who had been neglected by parents who simply had no emotional contact with their own inner children and therefore could offer very little energy to their outer offspring. The pain of this kind of emotional cut-off cannot be underestimated.

Then there were those who grew up with the deep wounds of the trauma of World Wars, Korea, and Vietnam. Still others discovered little children inside still bleeding from the experience of the Great Depression. The horrors of public education, boarding schools and military schools for the inner children are well known to people who explore the incredible world of the inner children.

Some people emerge from the above experiences in a more balanced way because they were encouraged to express themselves by those who loved them. Unfortunately, very few of us grew up in families that encouraged the kind of awareness necessary for a broad range of the expression of the many selves that are hurt in childhood. The blocked expression becomes almost as terrible as the abuse.

When the small child confronts the types of abuse described above and is not permitted to talk back, or to protest, or to express the feelings that go along with the experience, the primary selves that attempt to protect at the time have limited choices. According to my observations these choices are: psychosis, death, or splitting and dissociation.

Of the three choices, splitting off the wounded segment and repressing it out of awareness is the best of a poor lot. This splitting and repressing lays the foundation for a series of personality segments that are divorced or partially divorced from the usual controls of the primary selves.

This first layer of wounded energy often includes enormous rage at the abuse of power and the injustice involved in specific pain inflicted on the inner children. These rageful selves are not pleasant to be around, either for the therapist or for the client. Often therapists will attempt to "get rid of" this anger because of its unpleasantness. In my experience such attempts make things better in the short term, but in the long term efforts at expulsion lead to further repression. The key to the therapeutic handling of these segments is to remember that this rage was originally created by the child to survive physically and emotionally.

Such subpersonalities are quite alarmed if the therapist seeks to join with the primary selves in the goal of ridding them from the personality. They would rather be repressed than eliminated. Difficult as it may be, these first layers of the hidden selves must be acknowledged and explored. They must have the sense that the client and the therapist are there to honor the work of survival done by the rage and upset. Only in this way will they become convinced that the aware ego is capable of taking care of the more deeply wounded aspects that stand behind them on the progressionary selves.

Bob especially was skeptical of his own inner wounds and of others' wounds as well. He did not at first "believe" the stories of these inner children as they talked. They were, he imagined, just made up. But, as he heard the pain, he began to know something rumbled somewhere in the caverns of his and other people's unconscious. The experience of a pain that bubbles up to the top is the clue sent from the inner child. The red flag is the pain that surfaces as the aware ego listens to the inner children. When adults experience a hurt sent by the inner child, they can be certain that there is a real set of events that produced the wound. These inner children simply do not make up trauma. They have no reason to: There is enough terror in reality without a manufactured one.

Large numbers of people don't seriously consider psychotherapy or any other deep form of learning. They go through life having little hint of the inner pain of their children, except as their bodies eventually tell them, under the heading of stress related diseases, or as they carry around a low level of depression and/or anxiety. They have no hint of the profound inner wounds, but these wounds keep spilling out onto and ruining their relationships. If asked, they would have no knowledge of the jarring hurt of their inner children. But they can easily observe that "something" keeps them from having successful, intimate relationships.

Many other people participate in a restrained therapy or learning situation where the inner child is not allowed to speak, and, in this case, they too would not be aware of the inner wounds. Crucial to the kind of change and transformation that allows people to move to the next level of their own evolution is a safe context where the inner child can voice whatever is on its mind, especially its pains.

Jumping Mouse's experience with the buffalo offered some protection in that he walked beneath the buffalo's belly, some danger from the hooves, and much guidance toward the sacred mountain. These wounded selves require much of us through the pain that they bring, but they also are the guides that lead us up the evolutionary path.

THE UNFOLDING STORY OF THE INNER WOUNDED CHILDREN

Bob and Betty both received twinges of pain from their inner children long before they entered therapy. Bob constantly felt disapproval coming from other people, and Betty experienced a certain tension whenever she touched a man. As they listened more to the inner world of their subpersonalities, they found many aspects they loved to listen to. Behind these voices they knew and now respected, they could hear the vibrations of the hurt voices grow, and they didn't want to listen. None of us does. We would rather avoid and deny the pain.

Eventually, it dawned on Bob and Betty that the greater pain lay in denial and avoidance. Jumping Mouse eventually met the wolf who required the other eye, thus leaving him with the almost unbearable pain of darkness. So it is with our work with the inner children.

At first there is just a twinge. Years pass. Then, as the aware person gains more awareness, he or she inches closer to the pockets of pain, which have been far beneath the surface but which have been sending messages for years to the conscious surface in the form of anxiety, pain, shame, and guilt.

Increasingly, Betty noticed through her developing awareness that she felt uncomfortable around men over sixty. These older men at first appeared in her dreams as villains who victimized little girls. Through voice dialogue and other expressive modalities she talked to the inner little girls, and they told her that they had been hurt.

Then, one day, she had a brief flashback of her grandfather's touching her genitals. Afraid that she was just making this up, she got out the family photographs. There, she saw that he often was focused in his attention on younger female members of the family, not males and not his wife. There was not one picture of his touching his wife, but many of his touching her and her cousins.

Later, as she voiced some of her feelings to an older cousin, the woman confirmed that she had seen her grandfather fondling Betty in a sexual way. This book does not cover the scope of working through the wounds of incest, but it is enough to say here that Betty needed long conversations with this little girl who had been completely hidden from her for over twenty-five years.

At times the experience seemed to overwhelm her, to wolf her down. Yet, she courageously stayed with these conversations. Beyond that, she began to carry on a series of conversations with a budding subpersonality that was the parent—mother and father—to this wounded little girl. Crucial was the evolving relationship of these two aspects within.

The wounded self Bob found at the end of this particular progression was not so dramatic, but nevertheless painful. The subpersonality he met was a little boy who never got to play with his father because his father did not know how to play with his own inner children. Bob's wounded little boy was inundated by the sadness of spending a childhood with adults who expected him to be a little adult rather than a child.

It was these desperately vulnerable little children that lay behind the difficulties in Bob and Betty's marriage, and, as they became better acquainted with them, they could make their needs made known to each other. As they spoke more directly by channeling through an aware ego, the marriage improved immensely.

HIDDEN POWER AT MEDICINE LAKE

Jumping Mouse was most vulnerable as he lay next to the medicine lake, and it was at that time that he was hit by the eagle. The image of the eagle consuming the mouse is not a pleasant one, yet it is the fulcrum of the energy of the story. It shows us that the way to power is through vulnerability, not the denial of vulnerability.

One grandfather that I know well experienced the death of a son, and his grief would not pass. Already burdened by the death of another son in Vietnam, this tragedy threatened to ride him into the ground. Goaded by tribal politics and demonic energy, his son's enemies attacked and brutally killed him in the midst of a tribal ceremony.

The power in his work as a medicine man wained as the grandfather drifted deeper into despair. He was depressed over his lack of control over a senseless death of a loved one. Some of the members of his medicine society suggested a pathway through the grief back to his power. Their solution was a shocking one—his tribal friends buried him in sand up to his neck, where he stayed several days. They provided only a little water. The Sun roasted his face, but his guides would not relent. His tongue swelled and popped out of his mouth. His voice became a whisper as he cried out from the various subflows of energy that protested the injustice and insanity of the deaths of his two sons. His terror grabbed his stomach when even the smallest ant crawled near his face.

But still his friends would not dig him out: It was not yet time.

As he experienced his total helpless over the senseless death of a loved one through the explicit helplessness of being burined in the sand, his inner power slowly returned. Time and again, he would struggle against the sand and scream in agony to his friends to uncover him. Wave after wave of his grief surfaced, as he wailed and ranted in anger against them and life itself.

His guides remained impassive. They did not uncover him until together they agreed that he had cried out enough, until his complete helpless voice had been experienced in its depth, and until his rage had been spoken again and again at his condition, made explicit by the live burial.

The eagle power emerges through the powerlessness. From this acknowledged powerlessness arises a more substantial power that we will explore in the remaining chapters.

REFERENCES

Jung, C. (1977). *The portable Jung* (J. Campbell, Ed.). New York: Penguin.
Storm, H. (1972). *Seven arrows.* New York: Ballantine Books.

8

The Spiritual Selves

After the wolf left Jumping Mouse alone on the sacred mountain, Jumping Mouse experienced profound fear. He was blind, and he knew that the eagle would find him. The eagle discovered, killed, and ate him. In that way Jumping Mouse became part of the eagle. He had been transformed from an ordinary mouse bent on survival to an eagle full in flight.

Such is the direction of the transforming journey: from selves bound to the earth to selves that can soar in the heavens. At the same time the mouse is not lost or denied. He becomes part and parcel of the eagle, which in turn can never be the same once he eats the mouse. Notice that the theme of the myth is that Life feeds on Life to nourish Itself: The mouse gives up its eyes for the healing and transforming process. This giving up of the eyes leads to the next step of transformation. The eagle eats the mouse; the mouse becomes part of the eagle; together they soar.

CHRIST ENERGY AND THE SPIRITUAL SELVES

This notion shakes the foundations: the Universe feeds on Itself and in that way transforms Itself. Yet, on a closer look, it also offers encouragement. Jesus, to cite an example, gave up much of Himself in order to be raised to the energetic level of Christ.

This statement is broad in its scope, and it is not within the purview of this book to comment on it fully. It is enough here to notice that Jesus must have been aware of certain sexual appetities and other basic energy flows within. He must have been aware of the part of Him that wanted to be a husband, of another that wanted children, of another that wanted to be a grandfather, and of another that wanted to be a wise old man, to name just a few. The tributaries of these parts fed richly into the flow of His awareness, though they did not gain much attention from the recorders of his life.

He chose to listen to other parts that counseled healing, revolution, death, and living again in another energetic form. The aspects of Him that wanted to be a husband, lover, warrior, father, and grandfather gave up their lives for these nonordinary parts. With the nourishment of the subselves that wanted to be husband, father, and grandfather, the Christ Energy flourished and gained a prominent place in Jesus' inner lodge.

Did the Christ energy, the basic spiritual self within Him, take over his aware ego? From my point of view, no. Even to the last few moments Jesus processed various energies from an aware ego. On the cross He listened to the segment of Himself that did not want to die and also to the aspect that believed that this death was His destiny. From an aware ego position He chose a course of action that allowed certain aspects of His person to be sacrificed in order for other aspects to expand, as the mouse did with the eagle.

Even today millions of Christians go through a symbolic act called the Eucharist, whereby they "eat the body of Christ and drink His blood." If this eating flesh and drinking blood sounds primitive, it is— or, at least, was when it first began. The act is a remembering that Life gives up something of Itself so that other forms of Life can evolve and transform. It reminds us that certain aspects of ourselves feed other aspects and open new possibilities.

MUTUAL FEEDING LIFTS THE CONSCIOUSNESS PROCESS

In the Native American way, all life is in the food chain, and the plants and animals that we eat give up their lives in order to further the process. They then live in us, and the way we live honors (or shames) the ones we've eaten. In the same way that the eagle could not remain the same after he had eaten the mouse, so we cannot remain the same after we consume a particular creature, plant, animal, or energy unit from another person.

Eventually, we die, and the physical part of us then feeds the earth with our remains while the vital awareness energy travels, according to one tribal myth, along the Milky Way to the Ultimate Source, thus joining and expanding the Universal Energy. In this view of the world, everything contributes to everything and lifts the process to a higher level.

One way I have suggested that this inner nourishing of the individual takes place is through the expanding of the aware ego. The subpersonalities strain to express themselves. For years there is no aspect of the person there to listen, and then the ego begins the journey of expanding awareness by listening to the voices of the parts, hence the phrase—*voice dialogue.* When we listen to the observer and patient selves, the awareness level is then taken to the ego in an ever-expanding process. Then, the aware ego can better utilize the parts. This moving to a higher level of awareness is what I call the transforming process.

So it is with all of the subpersonalities: They give up certain energy forms to contribute to higher consciousness. As they transform to a higher level of consciousness, they become more co-operative and congenial with the other parts for the good of the human organism and ultimately for the good of all creation. In this way they appear somewhat more "spiritual," yet they are not what I am calling the *spiritual selves.* These spiritual selves belong to a different class of energy, but first things first. Before we delve deeper into what the spiritual selves are and how to access them, I invite you to look closer at how a subpersonality transforms and raises to a higher level of consciousness.

A SUBPERSONALITY TRANSFORMS

In the beginning Betty's critic energy dripped with the blood of its work; it had a dagger in its hand that constantly threatened her. It even told her she would be better off dead than living the way she was. No matter what she did, it was there to critize, so she would drink or medicate in an attempt to put it to sleep. Nothing stopped the critic, so she went for help. When she started psychotherapy, still the critic was there to tell her she wasn't a good client. When she entered Alcoholics Anonymous, the critic was there to berate her for not detaching enough or for not making proper amends.

Later, her critic learned transformational language and used that on her as well. She wasn't getting to her exciting vulnerable selves quickly enough or she wasn't being powerful enough. Her critic was even critical of her for listening to itself: "You shouldn't be so critical of yourself." Somewhere along the way in her childhood and adolescence the critic had gotten out of hand and spiraled downward in a vortex of darkening energy that wasn't easily reversed.

Slowly, though, her critic quit dominating her. It became assured that her emerging aware ego could help her, even parent her. Really, all the critic ever wanted to do was to criticize her first, so that the pain of criticism from the outside world would not hurt so much. If she told herself that she looked lousy as a teenager, what her mother or friends said wouldn't hurt so much.

As she quit looking so critically at herself (the mouse gives up an eye), she became free to look at other subpersonalities. As they got attention, they provided nurture that helped with any outside hurt that might arise. The critic energy gave up its old power of holding a dagger over her head by luring her to be self-destructive in a number of ways. With some people the critic energy subdivides, turns on itself, and offers this seductive advice: "Drink this or take that, and the other critical voice will shut up."

Even this complex quiets down as the critic energy becomes convinced that there is an aware ego worthy of guiding the organism. It slowly ceased to bully her and others as it saw there were other ways to protect her. The critic energy freely gave information about itself through talking with the aware ego, knowing full well that, by sharing this information, it was losing its hold on her.

The aware ego gobbled this information up and assured the inner children that they would receive new protection based on this new information and would not be criticized as much. Thus, life feeds on itself and is transformed through expanding itself.

Freed of its overwhelming task of criticizing twenty-four hours per day, the critic now turned to higher concerns, like a wide variety of discernments. These discernments helped in the overall care of the organism. For example, Betty got interested in running a marathon. Her new critic said, "Yeah, that's great, but don't forget about your tendency to turn things into compulsions." In this way a critic energy can help the organism discern subtleties between desires and compulsions.

Marv's critic energy also transformed and moved to a higher level. We once had a workshop in honor of the critic energy in an effort to make peace with the critic energy in ourselves. Marv made this comment: "I don't want to do away with the critic energy inside me. I want to take the teeth out, or at least its fangs, but I need my critic. By wrestling with my critic, I have come to realize that the critic energy is necessary for achievement, because it points out details that I would never notice without its watchful eye. I want a critic with good eyes and benign teeth."

At least from time to time, the critic can become a higher self, even with a quality of the spiritual, as in ethical discernments. This spiritual quality, however, is not its essential nature. It continues to have many other more mundane functions.

THE DORMANT SPIRITUAL SELVES AWAKEN

Other selves, though, are inherently spiritual: they hibernate within the person, just waiting to spring forth as a spiritual energy. Some are lively energies that want to lead us toward spiritual ecstasy; they love religious experiences. Some want to lead us to discern the meaning of life. Others prefer magical experiences, like Elijah on his famous chariot or Moses and his burning bush or Mary and her angels or Buddha by the tree.

Others remain quiet and like us to listen to the still small voice of God. Still others are quite extroverted and love us to tell their story to the outside world. Some like belonging and give us a spiritual charge each time we experience community. Many that are in my view the most basic, perhaps the most important, are nature lovers and long for stimulation by majestic skies, wondrous mountains, and rushing rivers.

I label these energy flows *spiritual selves* because, like our sexual parts, judgmental parts, and various other parts, they have a particular function. Their function relates to the "spiritual." They take us directly to the ground of our being.

What is this ground of inner being? I can only be descriptive, not definitive. It is that tendency toward balance—*demo-bo-kosee* as the Creeks put it. It is that ground of selves that the Navajos voice through singing. This Sacred Mystery is a single Being whose unfolding has become this universe, the Source of all living things.

A Navajo Singer (Medicine Man) once said to me, "We sing in order to restore ourselves to inner and outer harmony with the rhythms of Earth." The ground of inner Being is that Harmony. These spiritual selves have an innate interest in this Balance and Harmony. In this way they lead to a glimpse of Something Larger than ourselves, and this leading toward the Sacred Mystery is their sole function.

Other inner energies also point to the Sacred Mystery but have other functions as well. Another easy way to distinguish what energies are of a spiritual nature is practical, not theoretical. They can simply be asked about their identity when they are accessed through disidentifying with the ego mass. As they voice themselves through facilitation, they will reveal their nature. As with other subflows of energy, they will not come out to speak if the facilitator does not believe in them or if they feel unwelcome in any other way.

At one point in his early training Marv had a severe block against his own spiritual energies. He had grown up in a Baptist church and his Baptist energies were not welcome to his psychologist critic. There were other inner personality segments that absolutely hated this inner Baptist. The first time a spiritual energy came into the supervision room, through a case that another supervisee was presenting, this voice in Marv popped out, "All this spiritual talk is pure bullshit. It is bullshit because it has no place in a clinical setting. Plus, all this new age crap makes me sick to my stomach. I didn't put all these years of training in to get the same bullshit I got in Sunday School."

It would be several years, as you might guess, before Marv's clients would tell him anything about their spiritual quests. As soon as he began opening himself to some of his inner spiritual energies, his clients suddenly offered him new material in this area. For therapist/facilitator and seeker alike, listening to the voices of these spiritual energies leads the person to an encounter of the Higher Intelligence behind the wind that rustles through the trees at sunrise.

It is this Wisdom that prompts the eagle to wait in the high ledges of the mountain for a certain expected current, that allows him to ride it when it flows by and to release it when it breaks. It is this primordial wisdom that speaks to him, reassuring him that there will always be such winds for him and that there is enough wind for all eagles. Strange at first, these voices become more familiar, like the whispers of fantasies. The voices of these spiritual energies speak of important matters, things that seekers recognize they have always known.

The process of listening to these voices is not complex; it is as simple as standing on a dark August night to look at a full eclipse of the moon. It is the energy that expands the chest when you rest on the side of a mountain and survey a larger piece of the Whole. It is even the inner surge that comes when you look from a tall office building across the greenery of a city you thought was only ugly and concrete. It is as though the inner spirit nudges, "You thought it was ugly and hopeless, but look again. Look at our brothers and sisters, the trees, that reach up and draw precious energy down to those that scurry about. They do this all day; they keep you alive. Love them at least as much as your marketing plan."

A WARNING ABOUT SPIRITUAL ENERGIES

Certainly, Marv had good reason to be suspicious of his spiritual segments. He had experienced many wounds through the openings they provided. Before we proceed further, I want to offer a frank warning.

The first part of the warning is this: Our spiritual selves, the parts that relate directly to the Higher Power, grow out of the soil of this inner Being. They are to be seen and heard only as bridges to Something More; they do not speak with the authority of the Divine on all subjects.

Second, these spiritual selves provide very useful data to the aware ego for most of life's situations. However, they are not—I cannot emphasize too strongly—set up to run the human organism, any more than any other part can run it. They can provide marvelous input, but they will make a mess of things if they dominate the aware ego. If, for example, the spiritual self is in charge, it will usually not allow the sexual self satisfying expression, and vice-versa. Only the aware ego can balance these two energies.

The guiding assumption of this approach to transforming ourselves directs us not to eliminate the ego but to feed it with awareness. The helium of awareness lifts the organism so that it catches the thermals of the higher energy.

Thus, the role of the spiritual selves is to provide input through awareness to the ego, not to run the total organism. Some spiritual/religious traditions encourage people "to turn their lives over to God." Often seekers interpret this directive to mean allowing whatever spiritual self is strongest at the time to dominate the ego space, a process that leads to imbalance.

I certainly could understand where Marv was coming from in his "bullshit" remark about spiritual energies. At one time in my early adulthood, I tapped into a spiritual energy that urged me to take risks. At the time my aware ego did not know how to handle this powerful energy, so it moved in and took over my functioning for a period of time. The spiritual energy that presented itself to me from the depths of my unconscious was natural, free, winsome, and, therefore, seductive.

Before I knew it, I had sold my auto, acquired a motorcycle, and decided to live a life of faith. The culture of the 1960s cultivated this spiritual energy, but its limited effectiveness was soon apparent. This energy did not know how to balance a check book, and it had not looked ahead to see how cold it would be riding the motorcycle in the dead of winter. I woke up one morning with my bank overdrawn, snow in the air, and nothing but a motorcycle to ride. All the recreational bike riders had put their machines away for the winter. I could only look through fogged goggles at a few die-hard riders and wonder why I had sold my car.

Further, this spiritual energy was not equipped to manage other energies within. Like its counterparts throughout history, its management techniques with the unruly primitive energies was to selectively repress them. This particular spiritual energy that was dominating me at the time allowed motorcycles, hair on the face, and other accoutrements of the 1960s.

Beyond those accoutrements, it didn't have any interest in attending to the rage that was knocking at the door of the ego space or the wounds of the inner children. The rage was over the lack of safety for these inner children, who liked to ride the motorcycle on spring days but not in winter. They also wanted money in the bank.

Soon, I woke up to a return of awareness; the administration of this spiritual energy was a failure. It would take considerable therapy to pick up the pieces of this particular energy. For years following, I was quite paranoid when a spiritual energy attempted to get my attention. When I felt the knock at my door from a spiritual place, I would simply reply, "I know you. You and your kind had me riding motorcycles, trusting God, and eating alfalfa sprouts. Never again."

No domination of the ego space by any one subpersonality, even if spiritual, is useful, because that rule blocks the input of the others, thus depriving the ego of essential awareness. With these limitations in mind, we can proceed to ask two crucial questions about the spiritual selves.

How do we gain access to these spiritual selves and eventually even to the being energy that is the ground of all selves? What are some of the benefits to the organism if this access happens without allowing that energy to dominate the organism?

ACCESS THROUGH NARRATIVE

Certain types of spiritual selves, along with other subpersonalities, are brought forward into consciousness through storytelling. These stories might be spoken around a campfire as with American Indians; they might be referred to obliquely as with the Zen masters; they might be rabbinical stories; they might be hypnotic yarns by a therapist.

In the formative years of early adulthood, I struggled through the 1960s searching for spiritual moorings, as I indicated earlier. My office was on a main thoroughfare that led out of a typically bland suburban tract. Two or three times per week, just as the sun was drying out the dew, an old VW bug slid on the slag parking lot to a dusty halt. Onto the porch would bound a tall man of Native American background, his cheekbones jumping out of the sides of his face, his hair short salt-and-pepper.

First, he gave me a bear hug that left me coughing for breath, and then he would speak. "Let me tell you something that happened to me. Once, I was hiking in the mountains of New Mexico where I grew up.

We came to a ghost town where people had not been for years. These were the remains of silver miners. They came obsessed with silver. They died. I could hear their voices telling me this wasn't the way. I could feel their sweat and blood on the boulders. I could hear the voices of my people in the background behind the sweat and blood pointing me to the Spirit. I could hear those same voices in your teachings the other day. You are my brother."

Then he would shuffle his feet, look into my eyes, and roar off. I didn't know if he meant I was his brother in the search for silver or in search for Spirit. Maybe both. The next day he returned with another story, sometimes for me, sometimes for him, and sometimes for our chaotic world. His personal narratives never failed to draw forth significant energies in me.

ACCESS THROUGH CEREMONY

We are a society starved for significant ceremony as well.

Some years ago I participated in a gathering of medicine people from a number of different tribes: Navajo, Creek, and Delaware. From sundown to sunrise, we engaged in a number of healing ceremonies. At about 4:00 a.m. tribal members brought in a young woman of thirteen: She was ceremonializing her menarche. As she entered the tipi, her face fairly glowed with energy, as did her grandparents, who, despite their advanced age, had been sitting on the ground for nine hours.

For months she had prepared for these moments, and now, after considerable fasting, she stood before tribal elders and members of the medicine society. The chief of the ceremony, the medicine man in charge, spoke quietly to her about her ancestors, for he had been present as a young man when her grandmother had stood where she stood. He also spoke to her with compassion and respect concerning the divorce of her parents. Tribal members from her father's tribe were there, as were members from her mother's tribe. Her step-father's tribe also was represented. They all spoke briefly, giving attention to successes and failures of her clan.

Then the chief invited her to speak. Later, I discovered that her inner preparations had not included the knowledge that she would be asked to speak. She had no prepared text. For perhaps fifteen minutes she stood there speechless as to what she could say to her elders in a tipi meeting she had never before been allowed to enter.

No one made a move to help her. Her face was a screen that revealed a variety of subpersonalities as they came forth: a fearful one, an angry one, a controlled one, a shy one. Her mother rustled, and I thought she might come to her aid. But still her tribal people left her standing alone. At last, a light began to shine in her eyes, and she spoke. "The Great Spirit is now with me. I can smoke the pipe." She then puffed four times on the Sacred Pipe, coughing with its strength.

It was clear to me that the ceremony had called forth a spiritual energy that was new to her. When I checked this out later with her and her mother, it proved to be true.

The menarche ceremony happens once in a lifetime, but there are other ceremonies that are regular in their appearance. Bob and Betty grew up Roman Catholics and through the years had allowed a rebellious energy to dominate their religious life. Neither had indicated to me their religious heritage until, one Christmas, I noticed Betty humming a carol. Upon my inquiring about it, she seemed embarrassed.

I asked if I could talk to the part of her that sang the carol, and found it to be delightful. That aspect of her loved the liturgy of the Catholic church, loved the singing, and could still smell the church she grew up in. This inner segment still believed most traditional theology and wished that she would return to her roots to see if their was something there for her. This spiritual self conflicted intensely with a new-age spiritual self. She would have to sit in an aware ego space to listen to both of these voices and decide how to honor both of them.

ACCESS THROUGH THE VULNERABLE SELVES

A most impressive feature of these Native American myths and ceremonies is that they deliberately lead the seeker into the vulnerable. In the sweat lodge the heat and darkness call forth the vulnerable selves. In the vision quest the fasting and solitude in the wilderness call forth the vulnerable. In the above ceremony the elders deliberately allowed the young woman to stand alone in her vulnerability. They spoke tenderly but directly about the most vulnerable experience of her life: the divorce of her parents. At first, the vulnerable energies of fear and shyness dominated her. Yet, as they subsided, they seemed to prepare for a more genuine spiritual presence.

In the parade of selves in the process of transformation, first come the primary selves who do the protecting and posturing. Then come the first wave of vulnerable selves, the ones easier to face. Somewhere, there will be more primitive, jungle-like selves that can roar. Then there will be increasingly vulnerable selves that show up as they come to believe that the seeker can receive and nurture them.

They open the way for the spiritual selves that connect with the Higher Power and provide a Cosmic parenting for the vulnerable selves.

It is the intensity of the vulnerable selves that reminds us that our aware egos must call on sources of nourishment that are beyond the capabilities of our usual selves. It is the spiritual selves that become conduits to transmit the higher, healing energy to the vulnerabilities as they come forward. In many forms of psychotherapy, this latter stage does not happen, because the therapists are unfamiliar with the spiritual aspects of themselves. In those cases the vulnerable selves are greatly helped by the nourishment provided by the usual parenting selves, but they miss out on the larger resources of Mother (Earth), who provides us with the soil of inner balance and harmony, and of Father (Sky), who draws us to look beyond ourselves and cultivate inner awe, mystery, and gratitude.

ACCESS THROUGH LISTENING TO THE BODY

Just before we went into the tipi in the ceremony I cited above, an old medicine woman approached me, noting no doubt that I was the only non-Indian there. "When you sit on the earth from sundown to sunrise without leaving except to pee, your body will know it, especially when you are as old as I am. This is a hard ceremony, but I hope you will see it as worthwhile." The ceremony honored, among other aspects, a function of the body—menstruation. She was warning me that the spirit would come through the body.

In many traditions the way to the spirit is seen by ignoring the body or doing away with its desires. In this way of transformation, the body is honored and listened to, for it is the field of honor on which the spiritual and sexual energies, as well as other sometimes opposing energies, have chosen to meet. No learning experience—whether psychotherapy, collegiate, or religious—will be transformative unless the body is required to be there and be awake. Most deeply spiritual selves play hookey when the body can coast through an experience.

The spiritual energies that gain the attention of my aware ego are those that are interested in the substance of flesh, bone, fur, wing, scale, finger, foot, and brain!

ACCESS THROUGH BREATHING

In the course of her therapy, Betty finally came to memories of sexual abuse. As these intensely vulnerable aspects came to the surface after years of repression, they were accompanied by sobs and breathlessness. I invited her to breathe: first with her diaphragm, then her chest, and then through her nasal cavities. This three-part breathing is sometimes called yogic breathing, though it surfaces in many cultures, including Native American breathing. It not only draws out the vulnerable selves, it also draws in fresh air—life. It clears the stage of subpersonalities so that new ones can come forward. Eventually, it clears the way for spiritual selves to lead to a sense of balance and harmony.

ACCESS THROUGH THE NATURAL WORLD

The legendary psychotherapist Milton Erickson (Rosen, 1982) often had his clients climb mountains as part of their therapy. In the later years of his practice, a mountain south of Phoenix became a partner of his in the treatment process. He explained to his students that people learn something about themselves outdoors that they can't learn in. I maintain that part of this learning is the sense of Something Larger than oneself. Or, as one client put it, "Sitting on a mountain gives a sense of the size of my problems in the scheme of things. I feel something from inside well up that isn't ordinarily there; it is a part of me that feels God. My heart quickens and my butt relaxes."

This access route through the natural world to the spiritual selves is a royal road that has been travelled for millenia by shamans. In the last two chapters this access will receive more detailed attention.

ACCESS THROUGH TRANSPERSONAL EXPERIENCE

Transpersonal events are events that happen in relation to the universe that cannot be explained by usual reasoning. For example, once I was with a medicine man who claimed to have the ability to project himself outside of his body for the purpose of looking after someone in need. Through the several years of our association, I slowly opened myself to that possibility, though the scientific aspect of myself could never get on board with such a preposterous notion. Eventually, my aware ego has expanded in such a way that I can consider such possibilities while at the same time remaining intensely skeptical.

On one occasion we were out in the Big Thicket, a wild forest of East Texas known for its wild cats, alligators, boars, and snakes. Even wolves and black bears have been sited but not confirmed. A colleague of mine was with us and had not returned when we thought he would. The longer I waited the more worried I became. It was the middle of the night, maybe 3:00 a.m. The shaman in charge of the quest taught me a song in his native tongue to sing, explaining that, with these sounds, a person can follow the sound waves with a spiritual energy and observe the person to see if he or she was okay. He discouraged me from seeking my colleague with a search party.

Quite skeptically, I sang with him for a two-hour period, finally dozing off to the sound of an owl hooting over my head. While I was asleep, I dreamed in detail of my missing friend and saw in my dream that he was safe and sound, at first in his sleeping bag and then taking a short walk in the moonlight as it illuminated his features in an unforgettable way.

In my dream I wondered if I was dreaming or had entered another reality, a cousin of the dream world but different. When I opened my eyes, I knew my colleague was safe. This knowing came from a deeper place than if I had actually formed a search party to shine flashlights on his sleeping bag.

The next day, when my colleague appeared out of the forest in perfectly good shape, he was dressed in exactly the same clothes that he'd worn in my dream. Or was it some other altered state of reality through which I had seen him?

This synchronicity reaches beyond the grasp of my usual selves. They could not reason about this at all; however, they could raise all kinds of questions. I was grateful for their questions. I honored them. Had I seen my colleague dressed the day before? No, not in the clothes I saw in my dream; he had changed. Would I be able to guess at an unconscious level what he might be wearing, given the weather? Possibly.

In any case the transpersonal event opened the way for a certain kind of spiritual self to have a field day of play and fun. This spiritual self loves mysterious occurrences and miracle cures and in that way is useful. This spiritual self points out that there are many aspects of life beyond the realm of usual thinking, that there are connections and rhythms operating in this universe we can only guess about, and that creativity emerges out of these connections. This transpersonal spiritual energy balances the skeptic; they both offer something important.

As my native friend who told the silver mining stories would say, "There are no co-incidents in the world of the spirit."

ACCESS THROUGH DEATH

The nearer one comes to death through age and other experiences, so goes a tribal saying, the wiser he is.

Bob and Betty were concerned about their daughter taking a job in the Northeast with a large company. At the same time Bob was considering taking a new partner in his accounting firm, and Betty was considering going to graduate school herself. In the middle of the night, Betty awakened from a dream in which she had nearly died. Her heart was racing fast and she settled into the experience—what she called a feeling of death. "I was surprised," she reported, "that death—something I always considered repugnant—felt so comforting. As I would start to feel anxious about all the things going on in our lives, I would see death standing close to me. It didn't matter so much. A kind of peace came over me—something I can't explain. Like death was guiding me."

Early in her growth Betty was too terrified to listen to death, because she had other voices inside that were suicidal. She had first to expand her aware ego to the point that she could learn about the suicidal and homicidal voices. They were telling her to kill off certain ways of doing and being, but they were telling her in such a way that it overwhelmed her. As she grew in her capacity to hear these voices, they became less destructive. Now, in this dream, she actually could learn to listen to the spiritual side of death, the side that could open her to larger possibilities.

In this way death gives a certain perspective on an energetic level. What many aspects of ourselves strive after face to the background when death is near. As they fade, other spiritual energies come forward. They are the ones who say things like, "Hey, whether you make partner is not so important. Your son and daughter will be okay. You will die someday anyhow, and they will have to run their lives without your input." The nearness of death brings forth a quiet spiritual energy, one that is content with very little.

ACCESS THROUGH SOUND AND MOVEMENT

Most of the spiritual selves respond to sound, as do other energetic forms within. Eventually, Betty began attending Mass, especially on important occasions. When I asked her why, she responded, "Probably, it was the sound of the pipe organ that seemed to call me. That and the urge to sing the liturgical responses. Hearing the hymns that I knew by heart as a child drew this energy out of me that I don't want to deny." As for Marv, he acknowledged the segment of him that grew up Baptist by singing "Amazing Grace" along with Willie Nelson; this activity satisfied the inner Baptist and the inner Bubba.

The shaman uses her drum and rattle to gain access to a certain kind of energy. Here is how that can work.

After his first two vision quests where he himself quested, Marv participated in a vision quest as a supporter. While his friends and colleagues were out seeking their visions, he stayed with the pipe carrier near the fire to offer them support, as did many others. All during the night the drum beats in support of the quester as different supporters take turns drumming. So energized by the experience was Marv that he stayed up all night beating the drum. At one point he drummed in concert with another female support person. As the pipe carrier, I was awake every two hours to smoke the pipe and send special energy to the questers. Between these events I lay under the stars resting, and I could hear Marv and his woman friend playing. It was clear that they had drummed up a very sensual energy.

On and off he kept drumming, and at last the drumming drew out a spiritual energy that could actually connect with the questers. This experience surprised Marv, because he had a severe cold at the time and really had felt deadened by the cold medication. Yet the more he drummed, the higher his spirit self soared.

Once the questers returned, there was a dancing and drumming. As the others drummed, Marv danced the dance of the spider energy. The movements of the spider came closer and closer; it was an energy that was present at Creation, as the myth suggests. The sound of the drum and the movements of the dance had called this energy forth. It had been latent within him, waiting like freeze-dried coffee for the warm water of the drum and the dance.

THE MEDICINE WALK

After the event mentioned above, Marv began a daily medicine walk, a practice that had helped him immeasurably in pulling forth any number of inner subselves, including those with a unique spiritual flavor. I had talked about this experience to Marv when he asked me about a way to get oriented and balanced to daily tasks. This subject had arisen when we were talking about how unbalancing the work of psychotherapy is for both therapist and client. Marv was attending a sweat lodge monthly, but he yearned for daily practices that would help restore his balance; hence our conversation.

He first located the four directions in his backyard. He marked the four directions with the colors of yellow (East), white (South), black (West), and red (North). Each day, he would first stand at each medicine point and address the Higher Power Energy that comes from each direction, and then he would walk slowly around the circle.

As he walked, the primary energies he needed for the day would come forth. Then, on the next pass of the circle, the hidden energies would make their appearance. On the third circumference, he sought balance between the two poles of the primary energies and the hidden energies. The fourth leg of the walk was one of allowing the spiritual selves to come forward to nurture and guide him in the handling of these other selves.

These spiritual selves announce themselves by a trance state that makes the individual highly suceptible to the Divine Energy from within and beyond. These spiritual energies are to the Sacred Mystery what the sail is to the wind; they are present in the person. They wait for the subtle breezes that whisper across the waves. They wait for delicate energies that pulse into our lives from the Source. They pulse out of the early morning air and join with the inner sails, filling them to fullness inside. We cannot see them, but we know they are there.

You can become aware of these messages going back and forth between the Ground of Being and living creatures by walking in the forest. The natural world is attuned to multidirectional messages that flow back and forth. Just as the forest is a system of living information flowing back and forth, so are you. So am I.

Like the webs of the spider that are not seen unless the sun crosses them at a certain angle or they are filled with the morning dew, so these webs of messages that course between the Great Spirit and inner spirit are not seen or heard except under certain conditions. The access routes that we have looked at are barely suggestive of the trillions of connections between even the simplest of organisms. It is the sometimes joyous task of seeker and facilitator to stumble upon these hidden routes together.

CONCLUDING AWARENESSES

The resources of the spiritual energies are vast. At the same time, they cannot be allowed to manage life on this planet until the planet evolves far beyond where it is now. The survivor selves balance the spiritual selves, and the primitive selves balance both. At the center sits the aware ego.

REFERENCE

Rosen, S. (1982). *My voice goes with you.* New York: Norton Co.

9

Psychotherapist, Shaman, and a Feathered Buffalo

This chapter probes who facilitates the transforming process and what he or she does. What is the work of the facilitator of transformation? How do the psychotherapist and the shaman enter the process? Can they be one and the same person? Where are the models for joining Nature in the transforming process? To wrestle with these questions, join me as I dive into the pool of an experience that is fed by both the psychotherapist and the shaman.

Just before 4:00 a.m. I awaken to the flash of lightning and the guttural roar of thunder. It was the morning that I was to be the chief pipe carrier in a vision quest—a first for me at that time. Much of me felt well prepared, because I had been an assistant pipe carrier in numerous vision quests and had been conducting the *inipi* (sweat lodge) for seven years with the support of several medicine people of Native America. Other parts of me wanted nothing to do with this endeavor.

The pipe carrier (shaman) part of me was delighted with the storm outside. "Listen to the Thunder Beings," he said to me. "They are here to add power to the vision quest. Those who cry for a vision will be blessed by these Thunder Beings. It may even be the Thunderbird from the West. Listen to him flap his wings with the rolling thunder and speak with the sharp claps. He flies to honor your sacred pipe. Even as the storm calls forth the plants and the creatures, so it will call forth new visions and voices in the seekers. The Thunder Beings will bring the power you need for the next few days."

Another aspect of me, the overresponsible father, was worried about the rain beating against the window. The eight people committed to sit on the "mountain" to seek a vision would be soaked to the bone if this continued, and one of them was barely over pneumonia. With this storm maybe the eight seekers and their fifteen supporters would not show up at the meeting place because of the flooding.

Other segments of my being wanted absolutely nothing to do with this endeavor. They had not signed on for this kind of duty; they thought it was altogether ridiculous as well as intellectually unrespectable. They covered up a vulnerable part of me that was scared by the storm, and he won the inner battle as I buried my head under the pillow and went back to sleep.

While I slept, I dreamed:

"Judith Yost, my co-worker and spouse, and I are packing. We leave from some apartments adjacent to a park near our actual house. As I carry out the sleeping bags for the vision quest, a large bluejay hops near me. I can't believe how big it is; it is larger than a crow. Even more unusual, it is marked by yellow colors. I question whether it is a bluejay, but then I see that it is. I laugh to myself that maybe it is a 'yellow-jay.'

"As we approach it, it is not frightened at all. It shapes itself into a living sculpture. At first, I can't tell what it is, but then I see clearly that it is now a buffalo, a beautiful, yellow-marked buffalo with feathers. At the sight of the bird/buffalo, tears of joy streak down my cheeks.

"Then it transforms itself back into the usual shape of a bird and hops over to us and up into Judith's lap. It turns over and exposes its stomach to be scratched.

"I look closely and see that it has clear skin, so that I can see into its organs. We remark about how pure its insides are. Then I notice that it has a tag on its leg, put there by a wildlife program to protect it, since it is an endangered species."

When I awakened to first light, the vulnerable parts of me were nurtured and quieted by the dream. When they felt safer, the raucous voices of the subunits that despised my work as a pipe carrier also quit speaking. They didn't have any serious arguments against this dimension of the transformational work, but they did want to be able to stand behind my work. They had told me in previous inner conversations that they would not stand behind any work I did that was not of my own experience.

They had further told me that, as the protecting and conserving energies inside, they didn't want me doing any kind of transformational work or writing that I had not experienced directly myself. They had made a deal with me that, no matter what I learned from whatever teacher or therapist, it had to be confirmed by my own experience as being effective.

In something as important as this vision quest, they demanded an inner direction, because they would not settle for the direction of someone else's experience, no matter how much I might respect that person. This dream that personalized the myth of the Many Colored Buffalo seemed to fit the bill for them. In that ancient myth the medicine or transforming power is depicted as a buffalo changing from a brown calf to a white buffalo to a black bull buffalo. In this dream my unconscious tells its own unique version of the myth. In its version the change moves from the bird to the buffalo and back—a spiral of transformation.

As I walked deeper into the ways of the shaman, I found that my unconscious would take a myth or ceremony and send a dream that would be its interpretation of that myth or ceremony for me. In this way the personal unconscious will mark a myth or ceremony much in the same way that a wolf marks its territory with its own urine. The vision quest itself unfolded in the days following the dream as a remarkable transforming experience for myself and for the seekers who attended. The vision quest, along with the dream, fueled me to address these questions about facilitating transformation.

THE PSYCHOTHERAPIST AS ECOLOGY THERAPIST

The role of the psychotherapist, in my framework, is to guide the client through the crisis that precipitated the beginning of the therapy process. As the crisis reaches a manageable proportion, the client is faced with whether to go deeper and listen to the many voices that attempted to come through in the crisis, or to end the process. If there is impetus for this deeper work, the psychotherapist acts as a guide across the bridge away from the crisis to the deeper work.

In this next phase after the crisis, the psychotherapist becomes familiar with the survival selves and facilitates the client in separating enough from these voices to hear and see them. Later, when the shaman takes the client to the outdoors, there will be many dangers. The client must be able to employ these survival selves in awareness rather than overidentification. Alongside the separating process from these survival segments comes the ability of the therapist and the client to appreciate, even love, these survivors. This attitude stands in sharp contrast to approaches that seek to enter into battle with and overcome the "resistances" or "defense mechanisms."

Through group therapy and/or workshop settings the psychotherapist/facilitator of transformation introduces the client to the community as a forum for listening to these inner voices. This group work sets the stage for the deeper tribal connections that will be provided by the shaman both with Nature and with other tribal seekers. In the group work the therapist and client journey into the unconscious in search of various hidden selves, some vulnerable and some mildly instinctual.

As the transformative process picks up steam, therapists and clients reach another boundary. When clients cross this boundary, they see that the process is not just "psychotherapy" but a transforming process. It is evolution itself and reaches through all life, through death, and beyond.

Usually at this point, clients see themselves as seekers or sojourners, and psychotherapists see themselves primarily as guides. In traditional psychotherapy this time is usually seen as the termination phase of the therapy. Sometimes the therapy ends at this juncture because the client has not been able to make any connection with inner segments of the person that yearn for higher and altered states. Sometimes the therapy ends because the psychotherapist does not recognize the energetic vibrations of the soul that are crying out for facilitation and connection to the Higher Being.

If, on the other hand, the therapy has been sufficiently rich, the client will truly be a seeker after more. The hunger has just begun. The far reaches of peak experiences and deep valleys have not yet been reached. At this juncture a shaman is needed for the next leg of the journey, because the setting of the process moves from indoors, the domain of psychotherapy, to the outdoors, the domain of the shaman. There are yearnings in the deep recesses of the client/seeker for overcoming the estrangement from Nature. Many of the disowned selves that precipitated the original crisis cannot be reached until the client/seeker moves outdoors, where these disowned selves feel more at home.

At this point the psychotherapist refers the client to a shaman or seeks out shamanic training for the competence to take the client into this new and most important phase of the transformative process. Crucial to the process is the bifocal emphasis of psychotherapist/shaman, who combine to form a powerful *ecology therapy.* The synergy of these two currents of energy provides powerful impetus to the seeker.

FINDING A FACILITATOR

This whole subject raises the question about how to find a facilitator for a particular piece of work if the client/seeker has a sense that depth transformation requires a recovery of intimacy with Nature. Using the backdrop of my hypotheses, the search for a facilitator begins with energetic connections and then looks into whether the facilitator has a working awareness of the many interior selves. Further, a seeker should inquire early on about how comfortable the facilitator is in moving out of the office into the outdoor setting or referring to someone who can facilitate that kind of work, so that those inner selves that respond to the outdoors, primitive as they are, can be reached.

If the seeker begins work with a shaman, it is likely that the shaman will encounter areas of growth in the seeker that will not respond to shamanizing. There are certain inner voices that completely overwhelm shamans and, if they are unaware of their limits, render them completely ineffective in our culture. One shaman was involved in a complicated and basically negative bonding pattern in his marriage that resulted in numerous affairs. During these times he was prone to alcohol abuse and domination by a denial subpersonality that threw him into a state of disharmony.

At those times he lost his power connection and balance and thus his effectiveness as a shaman. In a herculean effort at awareness, his aware ego might surface for a brief period from this domination by the denial energy. At those moments he would know he needed help. Since he came from a very traditional shamanism, the shaman in him would not allow him to seek out a psychotherapist, which he desperately needed. He might consult another shaman, but the kind of work he needed was to reach his vulnerability, and the other shamans held him in such regard that they could not facilitate these vulnerable voices. Neither were they trained to be able to facilitate these voices.

Seekers, then, would do well to explore with shamans whether they know their own limits and their willingness to co-operate with a psychotherapist, because it is the synergy of the two traditions that creates the rich context of ecology therapy.

SHAMANIC TRAINING AND THE OUTDOOR OFFICE

The shaman is one who is trained in the ancient ways of Nature and can open passageways between humans and the sacred energies of Mother Earth and Father Sky. This wisdom comes from Nature itself but also is handed down orally through aboriginal traditions. I am not referring to outdoor knowledge taught by programs like Outward Bound or the like, though any acquired skills in the wilderness are useful.

Rather, I refer to the wisdom that comes when the individual leaps across the chasm separating modern people from the process of Nature.

When this bridge is crossed, the seeker enters a world where everything in the universe is alive and able to communicate with the seeker. The shaman seeks to help the seeker, not only to survive in a wilderness setting, but to establish energetic connections with the sacred mystery of Nature, spirit incarnate, *Wakan Tanka* in Lakota.

The shaman's office consists of the Earth, the Sky, the Trees, and all creatures, including what modern culture calls "inanimate" objects. To a shaman everything is animated, infused with some form of energy. Actually, "infused with energy" is not strong enough as a description. It is not as if we are a shell that is filled with energy; we—and the universal context in which we live—*are* living energy.

This approach might be called the new *animism* of ecology therapy.

The shaman understands the alternate reality where Nature seeks to offer voice and vision to the psychotherapist's client, and is the mediator between ordinary reality and alternate reality, able to provide the seeker a context where altered states of consciousness are possible. The shaman is not the source of these altered states of consciousness any more than the sailor is the source of the wind that moves the sail boat, but does know how to put the boat in the water, unfurl the sails, and be patient when the wind is not blowing. The shaman also knows what to do when the sails billow and thrust the boat forward.

Nature has taught the shaman the passageways into the deeper instinctual selves as they relate to the instinctual energy of the universe, and shamans are able to guide seekers in that direction. They perceive instinct, not only as a psychological reality, but as a transpersonal reality. They themselves have experienced, time and again, the tension between ordinary reality and nonordinary reality, the tension between day-to-day selves and primitive selves pulled forward by Spirit Incarnate in Nature. With the awareness gained through visions and listening to voices, like that of the feathered buffalo in my dream, they can make broader choices.

The shaman is the guide into the tension zone between these energies and calls it *Medicine Power. The shaman makes no attempt to escape from the tension of opposites both inside himself and outside, but embraces these opposites, sometimes in celebration and sometimes in terror, walking hand in hand with the paradoxes and contradictions with the full knowledge that the awareness that results from sitting between them is his or her power. Most of all, he or she walks with the tension between ordinary personal realities and Transpersonal Reality.*

On the morning of the storm, we left Houston to journey to the edge of the Big Thicket. As we bounced on strained shock absorbers along a dirt road, I slowed for what appeared to be a large rock. Upon closer observation, I saw it was a large turtle. I called this to the of one of the vision questers in the back seat who had traveled from the East Coast.

Why would I do this? In my medicine training I have been shown that the Living Environment will greet the vision questers, especially if there is need for encouragement. My more rational and conservative scientific energies do not like this kind of thing, but they also recognize the reality of these experiences. They have grown scientific enough to entertain experiences that are not from the ordinary sphere of reality.

This one quester had seen turtles around the world, and they had in fact led him to work with me on this pathway. As soon as I pointed the turtle out to him, he immediately knew and was deeply touched by this greeting, as was I. Immediately thereafter, a cardinal flew by the head of one of my clients, Pam, and I made a note that this could have something to do with her process and vision quest. This approach goes beyond traditional psychotherapy or even Eastern psychology, both of which focus entirely on inner or interpersonal energies. The shaman emphasizes the points of contact between the outer and inner natural worlds as they are enlivened by living creatures such as this turtle and the cardinal. In this altered state the shaman knows there are no such thing as coincidents; the creatures connect for the purpose of teaching and unfolding.

The part of me that would think this is ridiculous murmured a bit, but it had been worked with in the preparation that I had done and was content to rest for the moment, knowing that I would give it full voice at some future date.

In addition to the animal helpers, the ceremonies, myths, drums, dances and pipes are all aids in opening the passageway from our ordinary reality to the under and upper worlds where the seeker will have to journey in order to connect with the hidden energies necessary for this nonordinary dimension of the transforming process.

A fascinating and sometimes forbidding world awaits those psychotherapists who wish to learn shamanic ways for their own transformation and be guides on this leg of the journey for their clients. Some interpretations of the myth of the Many Colored Buffalo prophesy that non-Aboriginals are to take on these ways and offer a spearhead of the evolutionary spiral. This prophesy was first taught me in my training with a medicine circle of several different tribes. Later, I discovered the reality of the prophecy by living the myth and dreaming the dream I mentioned earlier.

A medicine grandmother of Kwehar-renuh Komatsi blood took me aside at a crucial period of my training and said, "Are you sure you want to walk this way?" Her ominous look made me question my certainty, and I told her so. She cackled forth a snaggle-tooth laugh.

"Surely you can sit with an old woman all night, and I will show you some openings." She sat all night with me on the Oklahoma prairie while a hoarse thunder punctuated her teachings. She introduced me through experience to her outdoor office, one she had worked in for nearly eighty years.

Through the night she looked younger and younger, even sexy. The storm and the night brought forth healing energies heretofore unknown to me as we worked with natives with cancer and heart problems in her outdoor office. She acted as a midwife for the birth of selves in me that could walk through openings previously unknown to me. I would have some amnesia about this experience until the feathered buffalo in my dream pulled these hidden shamanic selves for use in this vision quest.

IMPLICIT TRAINING FOR SHAMANIC EVENTS

My implicit training as a shaman began when I was a child where I was taught by the Medicine Teacher of the Kwehar-renuh Komatsi, the Llano Estacado Landscape and the Palo Duro Canyon. Most of this teaching was unconscious. Later it would be made conscious by the teaching I received from actual pipe carriers, including a seven-year cycle with a specific pipe carrier, and beyond that with a medicine circle.

Many psychotherapists have already had this general training without consciously knowing it through their connections with childhood landscapes. One psychotherapist who trains with me as a shaman had a powerful connection as a child with Nature even though he grew up in New York City; the connection came through a local park and trips out to the countryside.

Another person, a rolfer also in our training group, grew up with the mountains of Colorado as a teacher. City parks sometimes work as well as wilderness areas, and any person who has insects in his house experiences something of the wilderness spilling over into civilization with the attendant implicit potential for teaching.

THE APPRENTICE SHAMAN

In addition to this general training, there exists a very specific training process of an apprentice nature, though it might not be called by that name. This approach builds on but transcends the work of Mircea Eliade and Joseph Campbell; both of these men studied shamanism from a distance (Campbell, 1983). Their awe was awakened as they stood in the rotunda of the Lascaux cave in France and looked at the animals drawn by an ancient shaman. However, neither of these men entered a process of training to know experientially the dimensions of nonordinary selves available to that shaman who drew on the walls of the cave.

Medicine circles throughout North and South American laugh good naturedly at our attempts to learn these shamanistic ways without intense personal experience. As one of my teachers explained it, "We tell anthropologists and others interested academically only enough to confuse them or lead them away from our secrets. We reserve those secrets for persons willing to enter the fire and walk the pathway."

It is enough to say that years of preparation are needed for mastery, yet the apprentice model affords the psychotherapist a way to begin immediately. As soon as I began a seven-year cycle of learning, I could lead as a shaman in a few baby steps those clients and students who hungered to walk the path. The important ingredient, as in psychotherapy training, is to have regular feedback from experienced guides over a period of years.

PREPARATION FOR A SPECIFIC EVENT

Specific preparation for being chief pipe carrier for this vision quest began twelve months previous to the event. Each such event requires preparation, even for experienced shamans. Several potential questers had approached me about leading them in a quest, and I went to a wilderness area to fast and seek guidance from *Wakan Tanka* about this matter. It is an awesome responsibility, one which I had resisted until I had completed a year of learning for each of the directions—a year for the earth, a year for the sky, and a year for all living creatures. A series of dreams and visions came as a disclosure that carrying the pipe for this vision quest was a *Wakan* (sacred) task, and that it was time, whether I felt entirely ready or not.

Some parts of me, I recognized, would never be fully prepared for such an endeavor. They were the inner conservatives I mentioned earlier; I listened to them with rapt attention, because they have served me well. Yet, my dreams increasingly lent weight to the inner parts of me that wanted to take the risk of acting as shaman on this particular vision quest.

These dreams and visions differed somewhat from my usual dreams in that the animal powers acted as guides, as exemplified by the dream I had on the morning of the quest. These dreams and visions were of a profound instinctual quality and were often followed by actual encounters like the ones I mentioned with the turtle and the cardinal. These signs acted as sign stimuli that released deep inner responses that were born out of an inner readiness. The sign stimuli of the animal fit as precisely as key to lock; in fact, Joseph Campbell calls them "key tumbler" responses (Campbell, 1969).

Everyone who has been with a cat or dog in heat knows about these sign stimuli. The female in estrus emits an odor that is a sign stimuli that connects with males in the area; the sign comes, and the animal knows exactly what to do. Shamans learn to open themselves to sign stimuli that come from nonordinary reality and to be guided by them. On a cultural level these sign stimuli are myths, and on a personal level they are personalized mythological guides. They don't address the rational parts of the human but rather go directly to the primal centers of the nervous system, "central excitatory mechanisms" and "innate releasing mechanisms."

The shaman becomes more and more susceptible to "impression" or "imprint," as Campbell (1969) calls it. In the earliest human communities there developed a linkage between humans and landscapes, a profound *participation mystique.* In my personal training I found that over a period of years parts of me were progressively pulled forward that understood my deep connection with the larger ecology.

These parts were personally mythologized by winged creatures and buffaloes, highlighted by the feathered buffalo dream. They aligned themselves into a constellation of parts that I call "medicine power," or *Ahe-Chay-Cha* is Muskogee, *wichasha pejuta* in Lakota, *yataalii* in Navajo and *puha kut* in Comanche. They have the innate wisdom of my animal heritage that stretches back millions of years and comes to me through the reptilian stem of the brain.

Medicine is awareness of the tension that develops between the power parts energized by the landscape and the vulnerable aspects drawn out in the fasting and sweating. The medicine enters through choices made in the tension of this awareness.

These inner animals connect naturally with outer creatures, speak their language, and provide the shaman with wisdom not available in any other way. In this way the shaman develops a personal totem of energies; I will explore these totems in detail in the following chapter. In the months preceding the vision quest, these animals appeared in dreams and then in actual experiences. Often the visionary animal would send a message, and then the actual animal would confirm or add to the message.

One of my medicine teachers once told me, "When you want wisdom, you go to the wilderness to cry. As you cry, your power animal will appear to you. Sometimes it will be in a vision or voice. At other times it will be an animal from ordinary life that will take on extra-ordinary powers. In your way as a shaman, the One-Who-Is-Above does not speak directly to you. He sends His messengers, mostly in the form of living creatures other than human who offer you the ways you need for teaching and healing and guiding. This Energy is called *Tunkashila, the Divine Energy in its immediate presence.*"

For example, four months prior to the vision quest, I journeyed to a wilderness area in Texas to spend more time in preparation. While I slept on the ground near a beautiful lake in late December, I had a dream of an eagle. This eagle told me much about who was ready for the vision quest, what was needed in the support system, where the vision quest was to take place, and what my role was to be.

Later the same day, a large bald eagle circled over my head and made dives in my direction; it was the first time since childhood that I had encountered an eagle in the wild. His energy made a direct connection with my inner eagle, and the inner shaman knew how to follow their lead. In later dreams, the dream eagle joined with the eagle I actually saw to transmit power and direction for the upcoming event. *The zone where the outer and inner eagle join energies provides the context of shamanic wisdom.*

PSYCHOTHERAPIST AND SHAMAN DIALOGUE

After such experiences the trained psychotherapist clamors for air time on my inner stage to help balance out the shaman. This inner psychotherapist has a scientific dimension that requires reflection as a bare minimum on what the shaman proposes. He really would like thorough research, but, in lieu of that, he will settle with a few reflective points.

The psychotherapist noticed that the shaman uses auditory aids in the drawing out of various subpersonalities. The usual choice of sound stimulus comes from drums, rattles, sticks, or other percussion instruments. Chants and songs are also integral to the various shamanic ceremonies that promote healing and transformation.

In order to quiet the inner psychotherapist so I could proceed with guiding seekers into these deeper, instinctual voices, I had to do some research in a number of areas to find some kind of rationale. The shaman objected to this as undermining the process, but he got overruled. In the position of the aware ego, I had to take into account the validity of both points of view.

One brief example follows: Several physiological facts support the role of sound in the transformative process. The auditory tracts pass directly into the reticular activating system (RAS) of the brain stem. The RAS is a massive "nerve net" and functions to coordinate sensory input and motor tone and to alert the cortex of incoming information. Sound, traveling on these pathways, is capable of activating the entire brain (Acterberg, 1987).

The psychotherapist also raised serious questions about taking selected clients and students into the *inipi,* or sweat lodge. He has been an essential part of the screening process in helping decide who would benefit from these shamanic ceremonies, typified by the sweat lodge. He is not, however, content to do that work unless he has some rationale in his language about why it works.

I, with some irritation, explained to him that there was not a mountain of data on this subject. It is enough here to note briefly some of what he has found on the subject. The heat experienced in this ceremony can induce a massive systemic effect which includes rapidly increased pulse rate, nausea, dizziness, and sometimes fainting. It mimics the biochemical component to high body temperatures during fevers which reflects the natural reaction to toxins.

Furthermore, the sweat lodge may act as a sterilization procedure, killing bacteria, viruses, and other organisms that thrive at body temperature but are susceptible to heat. Heat directed at tumors has been an experimental treatment for cancer in approximately fifty medical centers in this country, including the one here in Houston. One serious hypothesis proposes that heat is effective in killing cancer cells and also makes the surviving cancer cells more vulnerable to radiation and chemotherapy (Acterberg, 1987).

The psychotherapist in me settles down somewhat when he digests this kind of information, but he also insists that the impulse to participate in such outdoor learning events come from the therapy process in a natural way. One surprise for me has been that people who not only have little experience in camping but also abhor the "roughing it" notion are often the very ones most drawn to this form of transformation. Even when their hunger for this kind of learning is apparent, they have to convince the psychotherapist in me that it would benefit them.

Here the shaman and the psychotherapist are in agreement. The shaman knows the many dangers that arise when a person journeys into the realms of nonordinary reality. There are the physical dangers of the heat, fasting, and wilderness. There are the emotional dangers of the instinctual and/or wounded energies in seeker and shaman that are called forth by these new connections with Grandmother Earth and Grandfather Sky.

SHAMANIC PROTECTION OF THE SEEKER

The psychotherapist has certain responsibilities for the safety of the client in matters such as confidentiality, a place to meet, time boundaries, and the like. With the shaman the dangers multiply, not only with the outdoor elements, but also with introducing transpersonal energies.

After I had completed a vision quest in the rugged Sierra Nevada Mountains, a woman told me of the contrast between this quest and one she had participated in two years before. The pipe carriers in that quest were from a warrior rather than a shamanic tradition and had encouraged the seekers in ignoring their vulnerability. She became disoriented, ventured outside her medicine circle, got lost, and nearly died.

Even when the Landscape is relatively tame, other dangers are there. I was coleading a vision quest several years ago with an experienced Native American pipe carrier. He had warned the seekers of the dangers of the quest. Among the seekers were several people trained in outdoor survival skills on a level that would make them appropriate wilderness guides. Not realizing the intensity of their altered state through the fasting and the energy connections of the medicine power, two of them decided to take a walk during the middle of the quest. One of them became so lost that he never found an expensive coat he had used as a marker, while the other was found wandering in a daze on a dirt road by a nearby rancher several miles from her vision site.

This disorientation occurs as the seeker encounters the lighter energies from the upper world and the darker energies of the underworld. The psychotherapist is trained to work with the inner and interpersonal energies, and the shaman is trained to work with the transpersonal energies. The psychotherapist is trained to work with demonic energies within; these energies are those selves that have been repressed by the primary selves to the extent that they have soured. It takes a skilled therapist to bring them through safely.

It also requires much of the shaman to work with the soaring energies of the upper world that want the person to soar, not only out on a limb, but often off the limb. The darker energies of the underworld, sometimes demonic, challenge the shaman. They will overwhelm both seeker and shaman if the latter does not know his or her own demonic energy as well as darker energy outside the human psyche.

For several months before the vision quest, I visited, through my third eye, the Landscape where the quest was to occur. Usually, these visitations took place in the middle of the night. My animal helper in the quest, the bald eagle, would take me there. He introduced me to the creatures of the area: the snakes, the beetles, the skunks, the turtles, the birds, the raccoons, the coyotes, the bobcats, the cougars, the poison ivy, and the fire ants. With each of these (and many not mentioned), I talked at length, seeking their permission to be in their area. After they gave permission, I sought their co-operation with those who were seeking.

I explained to them as best I could why each person was there. The purpose of these conversations was to enlist these creatures in the transformative and evolutionary process. Without them, we could have a nice camping trip, or even group therapy, but not a visionary experience. Also, through this power animal, I would visit each of the seekers, at first in an energetic form, but later, as the time drew closer, in their dreams. The shaman never intrudes in this way but rather offers support of the process through a facilitating energy. In this way and in ordinary reality, the seekers were taught how to protect themselves and encounter both darker and lighter energies.

Some creatures, namely the snakes of the area, did not respond quickly to the inner medicine, so I returned to talk to them time and again until I could feel a consistent rapport with them. This process brought me back again and again to my own fears of snakes, and the eagle power had to expand to balance out these fears.

One night around 3:00 in the morning, I felt a profound encounter with a representative snake of the area in my dreams. We were friends, and I explained to him our purpose in the area was for balancing our many selves with the particular ecology where he lived. He was cautious and reminded me of the unwritten rule of white cultures to kill snakes upon sight.

I assured him that we were not there to kill without permission but to join. He seemed to be the chief of his clan and assured me of his co-operation in this vision quest. Even though it was at the height of the activity of his clan in the area, he kept his word, and we did not see any of his member during the vision quest.

A few months later I took a group into the same area for another sweat lodge. Since I felt so at home there, I neglected to consult him and his kind. After we concluded our time there, I drove out onto the dirt road. There at the entrance of our vision area was a beautiful copperhead snake, perhaps four feet long, the largest I had ever seen in the wilds, blending in with the red dirt road.

He said in a silent language, "Don't forget that this is our home. You were here this time and did not consult me. I hope you won't make that mistake again." To emphasize his point, a few hundred yards farther I saw what appeared to be a deadly coral snake, frightening red and yellow stripes side by side emblazoned across his body.

He too spoke. "In case you didn't hear the copperhead, I will emphasize the point: We are your partners when you link with us. If not, watch out!"

The vulnerable vision quester obviously needs protection so that the Ecology co-operates with the process.

Some of the seekers continued in psychotherapy, so the psychotherapist in me worked in traditional ways to help prepare them for the vision quest. To this date this inner psychotherapist remains a thoroughgoing skeptic of shamanic activities, like those described above; but he no longer seeks to stop them. He is satisfied to offer a balance to the shaman. He sometimes is jealous but more often appreciative of the incredible leaps on the spiral of transformation that clients make in such events.

SHAMANIC PROTECTION OF THE FACILITATOR

A crucial element in the field of psychotherapy in particular and the so-called helping professions in general is the issue of burn-out. Burn-out, according to the approach of this book, results when the aware ego is dominated by a particular subunit of energy. The introduction of energetics and body work can aid greatly in protecting the facilitator through the process of enabling the facilitator to disidentify with the dominating subpersonality.

An important dimension of burn-out is the protection of the facilitator, psychotherapist or shaman, from the toxic energy released when two or more energy units interact in the synenergy of the transforming process. If a psychotherapist wants to promote transformation on the level that I am describing here, then he or she will have to enter a powerful energetic connection with the client/seeker. These overlapping energetic systems will greatly influence each other, and in some instances the facilitator will leave the energy field greatly renewed.

In other situations the energy charge in the encounter will leave a high level of toxicity in the facilitator's system; this condition will be especially true when the facilitator becomes more effective at journeying into the deeper worlds of the client/seeker.

Evan, a psychotherapist from another city who had entered training in shamanic work to expand his already sophisticated knowledge of the energetics of transformation, needed protection of a different order. He woke up one day dead tired and with the symptoms of a serious virus. He had been leading a sweat lodge for some of his clients and students for nearly a year.

He was not yet a pipe carrier but was preparing for a vision quest that would give him that resource. In the meantime he was meeting at crucial intervals with a psychotherapist/shaman to receive training and feedback on the cases using this approach. During that process he and his shaman supervisor had lost energetic contact with each other for a month due to vacation schedules.

The result was that Evan could have lost his life.

Through the sweat lodge and other journeys into the underworld, his seeker/clients had contacted hidden flows of energies that had soured into demonic forms. Evan had been very effective in facilitating the release of these energies, too effective for his health. His situation was just the opposite of Rebecca's; she had been dominated by an energy that made her vulnerable because she was blocked in the energetic process. Evan had tapped into pools of power beyond his imagination; he had a tiger by the tail.

There is a crucial stage in the sweat lodge ceremony where some of the toxic energy is carried by the sweat into the Earth for our Grandmother to recycle the toxicity and return it to the individual in a renewed form. During this stage, it is important to have a powerful sacred pipe that will produce an energy through the smoke that will carry another type of toxic energy out of the sweat lodge to the far corners of the creation, where it will also be transformed and returned to the participating individuals.

What happened with Evan was this: he was very effective in facilitating the sweat lodge, but he had lost his connection with *Wakan Tanka* that a sacred pipe can afford. When that happened, all of the toxic energy that could have been transported out of the sweat lodge entered his body. Soon, he was weak enough for the invasion of a life-threatening virus. Because of the vacation schedule, he had not been in direct contact with his shaman guide and did not receive protection for this condition.

Until he could complete his vision quest and use his own pipe as a protective agent, he took the following steps. First, he was to re-establish his connection with his senior guide on a more regular basis. A most important feature of this connection with his senior shaman was that the shaman would enter a pipe ceremony during the times that Evan was most vulnerable to these boundary disturbances between himself and client/seekers.

Until Evan could learn the steps for protecting himself in these shamanic endeavors, he would borrow energy from his teacher. Since shamans know about these energetic flows, this type of protection can be of crucial benefit as the psychotherapist makes the transition into the shamanic world.

Next, he was to take a feather from a bird that had been an animal power for him and fan himself after each stage of his work. He was to pay attention to the burning of sage at other times to use that smoke to carry out some of the toxicity. During the sweat lodge ceremony, he was to burn another plant and swing it over his head so that the smoke could meet the toxic energy before it entered his body.

Further, he was to take a pail of water and place it under a power tree for twenty-four hours in order for the tree to purify the water. After that, he was to wash his entire body with the water ceremonially after each day that included in-depth transformational work. Most important, he was to stay in close contact with his totem guide, the process of which I will discuss in the next chapter. Evan had learned the hard way, like so many others before him, that working in the world of shamanism requires an experienced guide for many years.

SHAMANIC LINEAGE OF EARTH AND SKY

One way a client knows that psychotherapy has concluded is that the inner therapist of the client becomes more important than the outer therapist. A similar statement could be made about the inner shaman; however, in the shamanic way the process is much clearer. The seeker often comes to the shaman through an animal, or early on an animal helper will come to the seeker. At an unconscious level the client always has this animal connection which provides an alternative connection with Mother Earth and Father Sky.

Then, in the vision quest, the seeker receives a first name given by *Wakan Tanka* through the landscape. This name identifies the seeker as belonging to a "clan." My noticing of the cardinal on the bumpy road to the vision area and how it flew over a particular woman's head offers an example. When she returned from her vision circle, she told me how the cardinals had visited her in many different ways. Out of the eight seekers she was the only one who had these visitations. Obviously, I cannot control such visitations, and it was clear to both of us that she had been "adopted" by them. She was now a member of the winged clan.

The winged clan is her lineage: the cardinals, *not me,* are her main teachers for the time being. Although I provided shamanic guidance, her primary connection is with the redbirds. This factor introduces an energy that changes any transference or other bonding pattern that is occurring in the psychotherapy. The main attachment is to a particular clan in the ecosystem, not the therapist or shaman. The positive or negative bonding pattern (transference) is still there, but the seeker/client now has a powerful connection outside the therapist/guide. It becomes a lifeline to new power; the central authority moves away from seeker/shaman to seeker/clan. *Clan* in this sense means a primary attachment to winged creatures, not other humans.

More important than the outer guide (shaman) is this inner lineage. My first Indian name is "Winged Medicine," and a subsequent name that I received years later is "Walks With Buffalo." These are two favorites of many. Typically, one receives a new name that corresponds to an emerging subpersonality that can be used by the aware ego for the next leg of the journey.

The shaman, like the one who gave me these names, is gradually replaced by the inner authority, until a dream like the one I chronicled about the feathered buffalo establishes a direct lineage with the Earth and the Sky. The dream confirmed my new authority. It was the feathered buffalo who guided me in the protection of the seekers rather than the memory of something taught me by one of my teachers. The feathered buffalo and other winged creatures are the messengers of O-nee-ha, the shaman who first visited me as a boy in the canyon. These inner shamans, moving in the mists of dreams and other inner landscapes, join hands for period of times with the outer shaman to teach. In the end the lineage with the inner shaman becomes more important than blood.

In a lifetime a shaman will receive many names, and it is the clans disclosed in the names that give authority, not the various shaman. During the training/apprentice process the shaman-in-training will often refer to his or her teacher; this is out of honor and as it should be. Later, mentioning such teachers takes a secondary role to the direct lineage with Sky and Earth and their image representatives like O-nee-ha. Whether a person has this kind of blood or that, or has been taught by this person or that, fades.

CONCLUDING REFLECTIONS

All day the vision seekers stepped with tired feet into the camp, their heads held at an angle of dignity and their eyes clear and calm. Together, we processed their visions and ate lightly, grateful for their safe return from journeys into the wilds of their souls. The afternoon lolled by with quiet conversations or power naps.

Then, as the shade of the late afternoon passed to darkness, the drum that had sent its message of support all through the quest called forth its brothers and sisters to gather for an evening of expression. Around the fire some beat white willow sticks together in quickening cadence; others shook rattles filled with seeds. A number brought drums out of tents that answered the large medicine drum in antiphonal exchanges.

Out of the smoke of the fire, the chief pipe carrier danced a dance of the bird that became a buffalo and returned to the bird. Spent, he returned to drumming. Out of the chants a tall woman leaped, then crawled, showing her lithe body through the movements of the spider. Then, another quester allowed his body to show us the sound of wings, and as he passed by the wings of the night, the eagle passed in our midst.

Was it the sound of an actual night eagle who joined the dance? Or was it a mythic bird from another energy system sent to encourage the quest? No longer man, he became the energy of wings. No longer woman, she became the movement of spider. Crawling and flying, the two moved in our midst, their boundaries melted with the creatures they danced.

One by one all of the vision fasters joined the dance in gratitude for their connection with their animal helpers. On Monday they would return to computers, to head large companies, to sell insurance or to courtrooms. But now for these moments they were wing sound, spider, buffalo, wren, white bird, star, or bumblebee.

Their adoption by the animal kingdom was secure. They danced their tie to the tribe. Soon, they would realize their primary teacher was the Landscape. The psychotherapist and shaman were only a small part of that Natural Process.

REFERENCES

Acterberg, A. (1987). *Shamanism* (S. Nicholson, Ed.). Wheaton, IL: Theosophical Publishing House.

Campbell, J. (1969). *Primitive mythology: The masks of god.* New York: Penguin.

Campbell, J. (1983). *The way of the animal power. Vol. 1. Historical atlas of world mythology.* San Francisco: Harper and Row.

10

The Totem of Selves

The Buffalo Woman appeared out of the swirling smoke of a fire that we had built to heat rocks for a vision sweat lodge. The fire had died down to coals and green aspen as I sat alone in those pregnant, mysterious hours between midnight and first light. The others, who also supported the questers, slept under stars with Taos mountain air for a blanket.

She spoke through eyes that were like dark charcoals in the smoldering aspen; her voice was accompanied by a mother coyote in the background: "I came long ago to the Lakota. The two islands you call the Americas, especially the Island of Turtles to the north, had the spirit to bridge to spirit. At that time these people and that place were the most receptive on the planet.

"I taught and they learned.

"Then, the fire died to an ember, like the fire you look at now. My brother and sister buffalo faded to almost nothing. People—red, white, black, and yellow—came to this island as I had prophesied long ago. They came, but they took an alien path by raping the land, the creatures, and the trees. After that, it was predictable that they would turn on each other through fighting and slavery, and even the natives of the land joined them.

"They didn't know that, by tearing the heart out of the forest, they were tearing out their own hearts. They didn't realize that, by killing off the buffalo, they were killing off their own life blood. They would find other sources of food, but it would not be the same.

"Five hundred years passed. It was a time of turbulence and of gestation.

"Now I come to you tonight and to many others.

"The time is now ripe for you to hear the voices of all creatures.

"These voices will teach you, lead you on the way to expanding, lifting your consciousness.

"I am from the Giver of Visions.

"Before, I gave visions to Moses on the mountain, to Jesus in the desert, to Buddha by the tree, to Sitting Bull on the plains, and to Quannah Parker in the canyons.

"Now, I give to first a few, then to many, then to all, just as I have prophesied through many tribal traditions.

"The day of exalted chiefs is over. The time of many leaders who share their power is here. Small tribes will abound, and they will know their leaders by their willingness to share their power and acknowledge openly their weaknesses.

"The embers you see in the fire will become a fire that will light the consciousness of all the earthwalkers.

"This fire will be spread by the energies of all living creatures.

"The fire will grow as it spreads, first by creatures on four legs, then by winged creatures, then through you two-legs. Slowly, you will recognize that all creatures dwell within a unified field of shared consciousness. It will come to you that all is a projection of a single being and that all of us—birds, rocks, mammals, minerals, microbes, subpersonalities, and people—are individuated segments of one conscious and coherent Whole.

"This you have known for a while in the shallows of your being, but now I'm opening the way for this awareness to move to your depths, yours and others.

"Listen for the sound of wings and the thunder of unshod hooves.

"Look for my images in your dreams and visions.

"My gentle creatures will adopt you, then lead you, then turn you over to another creature to lead you on another step of the pathway. This leading by them will teach you that you are here not to dominate but to co-operate.

"These tiny insects and mighty animals will lead you out of stagnation to regeneration.

"Other two-legs will be listening to my voice in other forms. You are not to see them as threatening because they are different. You will know them because of their respect and reverence for all creatures.

"Many two-legs will have feathers in their hair, on their ears, in their cars, and around their houses. Others will carry bones, quills, rocks, minerals, and twigs that connect them to the creatures that lead them at the moment.

"When nonhuman creatures come, as they come even now to the vision quester who sits out on the mountain, you are to see them as they are. Observe them. Learn their ways. Read about them. Sing about them. They will speak to you and lead you by the way that they relate to their environment."

I stirred the fire and shifted the blanket draped over my shoulder. It was not yet time to smoke the pipe and pray for the questers, so I asked a question of the Buffalo Woman, whose eyes flashed out of the fire. "How will I know these creatures? What is their role in my life?"

"They will speak by coming into your life, crossing your path at a crucial, unexpected time. These intersections will carry a transforming charge.

"They will speak by coming to you and other earthwalkers even as I come to you now.

"They will be with you as you dance with them to honor their willingness to share life with you.

"They are beings from Being.

"When their time with you passes, another creature/image will bob to the surface of your consciousness, as if out of nowhere, even as I am doing now.

"This inner creature/image will connect with actual creatures in outer reality—its kin outside you.

"To show you how this happens with all people, a buffalo will come to you, because I need such to commune with me as I live in your consciousness. Together we will talk.

"You will hear, eavesdrop. What we say you can take with you as your personal wisdom.

"The line between your spirit and sacred spirit will have tiny holes in it, punctured by the beaks, the claws, and the teeth of creatures like us.

"We too will learn from you. Together we all will be lifted to a higher plane; the high planes you have sensed in your bones since childhood will now become a camping place.

"Just as I am Transforming Energy, so are you. Just as I move from two-legs to four-legs, so will you.

"Just as I go from reddish brown, to white, to black, so will you.

"Just as I kneel to the four directions to receive the Single Source, so will you.

"Just as I disappear at the edge of the horizon to return to this Source, so will you."

The memory of this encounter came after a period of amnesia about the experience that had lasted for one month. It unfolded, and its roots reached back into hundreds of childhood campfires. The memory of it flashed back into my mind as I journeyed to the ancient grounds of the Iroquois League on a late summer morning. It came upon me like an August thunderstorm, brief and intense as it beat upon the poncho of my soul.

It was startling in its vivid features as it dominated my inner stage for about an hour. I was aware of the energy, yet I had very little control both when it happened and when it poured out onto the paper. It was as if the vision and voice had been attempting to gain the attention of my aware ego for some time, but had failed. It poured forth, by-passing my usual ego functions.

Was it a hallucination? Was it the harbinger of a psychotic breakdown of my personality? Was it wisdom or craziness? The boundary between those two, as you well know, is not always clear, and I could only feel my way along. When I returned to an aware ego state, I experienced a skeptical and evaluating energy coming forward.

For me, wisdom, yea intelligence, is measured by the energy provided for the living unit to interact creatively with its environment. I would apply this measure to the vision, and I soon found that this vision/voice held much promise in my interacting with my environment. The Buffalo Woman who became the Many Colored Buffalo seemed to lead to the experience of the totem of selves.

Here is how I have explored that.

ANCIENT TOTEMS

In the ancient world a totem was an animal, plant, or other object that served as the emblem of a family, clan, or tribe. It was often regarded as a reminder of its ancestry. A bear clan, for example, might have as its ancestor an ancient bear, and bear energy might lead it in hunts and other adventures. It might be disclosed to the clan that it had several creatures that were related, and in some cases the clan would carve these creatures into a felled tree, something we call a totem pole.

These poles, especially among the Tingit and Skittagetan language families of northwestern North America, represented family lineage, often interspersed with references to mythical or historical incidents. They were placed in front of the tribal dwelling places as symbolic reference points to offer guidance and strength on personal and communal journies.

CURRENT CULTURAL TOTEMS

In our contemporary world we continue to use totems. Many of our athletic teams have animal emblems, totems if you please: bears, cardinals, blue jays, cubs, bulls, hawks, timberwolves, wildcats, wolverines, and so on. Some people drive their automobile totems as in a bronco, a cougar, a mustang, or a thunderbird.

The energy of these totems is mostly unconscious, yet advertisers continue to recognize the power of these symbols and their ability to attract two-legs. Totem symbols that are primitively related to animals tend to emerge out of the unconscious of American advertising executives more so than of their counterparts in cultures more removed from their primitive origins, like Germany and Japan. Yet even the refined British produce a luxury "totem" with a Jaguar on its hood.

The totems operate, sometimes powerfully and sometimes weakly, at the edge of our awareness. They largely are disowned energies, waiting to be embraced; in fact, the whole totem experience lies just below the surface of our awareness, straining to burst forth in a new flowering that offers incredible possibility in personal and global transformation.

The vision of the Buffalo Woman made that apparent to me.

CHILDHOOD ENCOUNTERS AND PROCLIVITIES

As children, we were particularly predisposed to accessing the world of living nonhuman creatures. Most children gravitate toward the totem experience through their natural subpersonalities. They generally remain rooted in this totem experience until later subpersonalities take over the steering wheel of the person.

In the backyard of my childhood grew an old pear tree that patiently educated me in many ways; it was an early totem, though I didn't know what to call it. I just loved it. Its limbs boosted me up as I climbed and sat in its wise old arms, looking at my world from a different vantage point. Its fruit fell to the ground, and I ate it joyously.

It told me eloquently that the source of my nourishment was not only my mother's breast or, later, the family refrigerator, but also the bosom of the Earth that could provide. Its fruit attracted wonderful creatures, especially butterflies. Gentle hours were spent with these extraordinary creatures as they would light on my shoulders, telling me childhood secrets I had long forgotten until this pathway began to open up.

What child has not lain upon the earth and looked at the cloud formations in the sky? The Rorschach value of this experience is well known, but the Buffalo Woman seemed to explain that the projection was not all one way. She instructed that we are living energy systems that interact naturally with the clouds, and that the clouds are living energy systems in themselves that project their energy into our energy fields, just as we do theirs.

A child, lying on the earth looking at cloud formations, takes something of the cloud with him or her, and the cloud takes something of the child to spread it across the countryside. There is, according to quantum physics and the totem way, an actual exchange of energy.

Even as you read, you may see clouds in your mind's eye, and these clouds may not just be from childhood. They are from cloud formations perceived in recent times that entered your consciousness. They are not just faces made in play, though they are that. They are swirling masses that move in circles and speak of possibility and nourishment; they continue to give energy to you as you think about them.

Not only do children lie on the earth, they also dig. Children are drawn to put their fingers in the cool earth, especially on warm summer days. Sand piles on beaches and rivers and playgrounds pull the child to sit, dig, and shape. This shaping of the earth is a voice dialogue of inner selves that come to the surface and that are there for the child to look at in the form of these shapings. This digging in the earth becomes the foundation of the totems that are already emerging both from inside consciousness and from outside in the trees, butterflies, and other creatures.

Children love to have adults read about totem accounts that we call fairy tales. These accounts include stories, sometimes profound myths, about the adventures of two-legs with wolves, pigs, billy goats, bears, dragons, snakes, mongooses, black birds, and many others.

THE REPRESSION OF NATURE TALKING

Most childhood observers agree that a profound repression occurs in the child between the ages of three and six, maybe seven. Freud's (1966) lens tells us that this repression is the result of the child's fear of retaliation from the parent of the same sex when he or she feels labidinal (sexual) feelings toward the parent of the opposite sex. His lens, though helpful, is not wide angle enough for me.

From the dreams, memories, and experiences of my clients, students, and my inner selves, I identify this repression as a result of forcing the child into the general confines of civilization. The sexual repression, though real, is just a tiny part of this squeezing process. This wider restriction takes the form of binding the barefoot in a shoe, of limiting the place of body elimination, and of discouraging physical movement. Expression of a wide range of emotion, of creative and unusual thoughts, of spiritual yearnings, and of idyosyncratic behavior also come within the restricting purview of the family, day-care centers, kindergarten, and other taming institutions.

This repressing movement in the personality and culture shuts off the channels between the person and the wilder environment, thus resulting in the nodal point of the human tragedy—our alienation from our natural environment and from our natural tendency to communicate with Nature.

It is, according to my hypothesis, this repression of the natural instincts toward connecting with the planetary context that results in a lion's share of symptomatic behavior in humans. I am not just speaking here of the instincts that are psychologically real for the individual, but also of the instinctual energies of the Universe Itself that reach out to connect with the inner instincts. The repression that evokes the most profound symptoms is the one which blocks out the dialogue between inner instinctual energy and outer instinctual energy through the creatures.

If you take a jungle cat and put it in a zoo environment, it most often will develop some kinds of nervous behaviors. If you don't balance a human's civilizing environment with outdoor qualities that include intimate contact with creatures, emotional and physical disorders will develop. *Balance* and *harmony* are the key words here because returning to the "innocent savage" state is not the thrust of this hypothesis; rather, the emphasis is on hearing both the internal voices that were civilized and balancing them with hearing the internal and external voices of other living creatures.

For years Bob would break down in tears when he returned from certain vacations. Through our work together, he at first talked to selves that did not like to return to responsibility in his office and at his home. This dialogue helped, but the next year the same sadness broke forth as he drove home from a Colorado ski trip. As he talked to that part of himself that was so sad, it spoke haltingly of not wanting to leave the outdoors, the skies, the freedom of movement, and the loose clothing. The profoundity of this statement did not dawn on either one of us at first.

Then this voice traced its feelings back to the first day of public school. It identified itself as a six-year-old little boy with a burr haircut. He told Bob's aware ego of the terrible feeling of being forced to attend public school, of the grief he was still experiencing over the loss of days free to roam in the backyard and nearby greenspace, and of the loss of being with frogs, yellow jackets, and birds. He told of long conversations with his dog, the pony he used to ride, the cat, and the ants in the antpiles. He told him how secure he felt within the confines of the wild crab apple tree in the vacant lot next to his house.

The creatures of this vacant lot were his friends. Not only was he forced to attend a school that restricted his movement, he also was taught there that creatures did not talk. The energies that he encountered were explained to him as "imaginary friends." Most of the important experiences of his life were now called "imaginary" while the experiences that constricted him were called "reality." As he became more socialized as a male, his friends and he shifted their consciousness. Instead of feeling friendly and talking to nature, they adopted the dominating energy of their culture. This domination took the form of torturing the animals instead of listening to them. This dominating, torturing energy soon crowded out the energy that could talk to and understand the creatures of Nature.

No person had taught him to commune with Nature; he had done that naturally, as do all children. Bob was taught to distrust this intuitive ability with which he was now conversing. This repressed aspect explained to Bob how lonely he had been, because Bob's primary energy would not allow him his friends from Nature.

When Bob would go on vacations where there was extended contact with the outdoors, he would begin to feel himself rousing with new life, perhaps even to listen to the voices of the creatures. Just about the time he would feel hopeful inside, he would force himself to return to the cubicles and the ties around the neck that this six-year-old hated so much.

So it was not only that this more natural segment of Bob was sad the vacation was over; he was also sad that he had to return to a world where he was not welcome, to a world where Bob's aware ego was dominated by energies that had developed in the early years of schooling. These subpersonalities saw no use for him. He was an unrealistic part that heard the voices of Nature.

As I participated with Bob in this therapeutic endeavor, I refined the hypothesis that the greatest loss of childhood is not the dawning realization that one cannot have the parent of the opposite sex all to oneself. The far more profound loss is the loss of Mother Nature, the loss of contact with the many voices that our Mother the Earth uses to enlighten us, and the repression of the portions of energy inside that yearn to talk with our many nonhuman brothers and sisters.

Our repression of this totem experience results in film themes where "alien" creatures burst out of our stomachs, humans become wolves, vampires seek blood, and sharks come out of the depths of the water. These themes speak, sometimes eloquently and sometimes crudely, of how our primitive energies long to contact the outside animal world, and of how this energy sours into the demonic when it is thwarted.

Because the most powerful connection that a human being can have is with Grandmother/father Nature, the inner subpersonalities needed to repress this contact develop an incredible defensive, even destructive, force. Most of our inner budget is devoted to the defense against and the domination of the inner urge to contact Nature. The enemy, according to these repressive energies, is not primarily the parent of the opposite sex but the Energies of Grandmother Earth and Grandfather Sky.

In 1969, when the U.S. first landed on the moon, my best friend was a key member of the NASA space team. We stood outside the night after the landing, looking at a beautiful moon. He spoke. "She is no longer a virgin; we have taken her cherry. We have won the battle. What a feeling!"

From my point of view, this voice that was talking in him was not the voice that wanted his biological mother conquered; it was far more profound than that. It was a voice that had learned too well to overcome Nature. It was a voice that had learned to shout so loud that it could drown out the inner and outer voices of Grandmother Nature that he had heard so clearly as a boy. It was the same voice that would grab a small kitten and hold it angrily, even throw it across the room because it was reluctant to be controlled.

It was a voice that would drown a cat because the cat would not submit to its control. It was a voice that would seek out snakes to kill because the snakes were seen as enemies that needed to be killed on sight by every "civilized" person.

I knew his voice well because I knew that energy in me.

This repressive voice that fights to control nature is needed on a very limited basis, but in our culture it is now totally out of control. Its repressive hand can be seen moving across the planet as it seeks the throat of our Mother Planet. The incest rape is complete, only it is the planet we rape, not our mothers. The throat is next. Our outer defense budgets will not shrink until we locate the real target of repression: conversing with the Natural Order.

Our drug problem is at once an effort to replace the highs that only our connection with the Higher Energies of Grandmother Nature can provide, and also an effort to anesthetize the inner voices that yearn to connect with their brothers and sisters outside themselves. Bereft of the inner surges and boosts that come from connecting with the energy of the Natural Order, we turn to drugs.

But they fail us.

Ripped away from the natural connection with their environment, Native Americans sought their visions in alcohol. Even the most casual observer can behold this condition, but we have not seen how nonaboriginals are going through a similar experience. So fogged by our dependence on drugs, air conditioning, starched shirts, and automobiles are we that we cannot know the source of our depression and sadness. We too have been robbed of our birthright, our pulsating connection with our Mother, the Earth, and our Father, the Sky. Torn away from the source of nourishment that emerges when we know intimately Grandparents Earth and Sky, we try to stuff ourselves with a truckload of junk food and then vomit it out.

No wonder Bob became sad and depressed to return from his vacation to an unbalanced life where the civilized energies squelched the primitive ones.

PREPARATORY ADULT VISITATIONS

Fortunately, the deep veins of Natural Energy cannot easily be cut off from the surface even after years of cultural and familial repression. In adult years they struggle to gain the attention of the person in a variety of ways. Dreams are one channel, but many dream interpreters, not familiar with shamanic ways, miss these dreams as the beginning of a totem.

Marv brought the dream of one of his clients, Sheldon, to our training group. Because of his own experiences with the spider, he thought this dream might have special significance for the awakening totem in Sheldon. In the dream Sheldon found himself in a cave. Water entered the cave, and so he had to crawl up on the side of the cave like a spider man. He was safe, but others in the cave were not. Next, he found himself outside the cave, talking to a man smoking a cigar in a red Cadillac. From that experience he figured out he needed to go back into the cave, even though he was frightened of the people running back and forth on the floor of the cave.

As he entered the cave for the second time, he found that he was crawling on all fours. He began to feel like an animal, and he no longer was frightened. To the contrary, he started to howl like a wolf. His howl felt good and strong, so strong that the people on the floor of the cave took notice of his power. It felt wonderful to howl, and he woke up to the tug of his wife's hand. She told him that he was howling in a voice that scared her.

He laughed and laughed. When he told Marv about the dream, he howled again. It felt good, he explained, but it wasn't as loud as in the dream. What further captured Marv's attention was that Sheldon was an engineer whose profession dictated against such outbursts.

As Marv and I worked together on this dream with Sheldon, the three of us recognized that this inner wolf was howling in an attempt to connect Sheldon with an outer animal. It was the first rustling of a connection that would later give him his first totem, an animal that would guide him in many ways.

The dream offered much material for a traditional interpretation, but the meat of it lay in the howl, as Sheldon explained it. If he had viewed the wolf only as a symbol of repressed sexual energy or even as a subpersonality, he would have missed a very important dimension. He would have missed that the wolf was attempting to lead him to connect with an animal guide outside himself. Herein is how this kind of work differs dramatically from traditional psychotherapy. The totem experience links up the inner subpersonality with an actual animal outside the person so that there can be another kind of dialogue. That would come later for Sheldon now that Marv had helped him understand what was happening.

Another psychotherapist receiving cross-training in the shamanic ways of the pipe carrier, Lee I will call her, told of an early attraction to whales. This innate attraction represents another conduit to the Natural Order. When she heard their sounds on the albums of the sixties, she felt attracted to them. After several years of sparse contact, she and her mother decided to take a trip together. Lee chose a whale-watching cruise without consciously knowing why she felt pulled in that direction.

While on that cruise, she was actually able to touch a gray whale as the whale came next to the boat. She was still in her twenties but had suffered much tragedy through the death of her father and her husband. Because of the intense pain of those wounds, she had turned her life over to subpersonalities that shut off most of her awareness.

She lived in numbness.

The touching of this whale awakened something in her. At the time of this early visitation, she did not know why the whale was important to her or why she continued to dream about the whale. She joined the "Save the Whale" movement but couldn't access its meaning; it would be nearly twenty years later before she could decipher the importance of touching this gray whale, as we shall see later.

Others have collections of shells and rocks in their homes that they have gathered. Sometimes the rocks are beautiful, but often they are very ordinary. Why do they bring them home? Why do they keep them? Numerous explanations suffice, but I see it as an early visitation from a living energy of the planet attempting to connect with us humans.

These visitations, according to the ways of the shaman, are the foundations of the living totem.

VISITATIONS DEVELOP INTO ALLIANCES

When the human seeker displays enough awareness, these visitations can develop into alliances. Usually, the creature will appear to the seeker under circumstances that feels charged with opportunity for learning. What distinguishes these developing alliances is the awareness in the seeker that something more is involved.

A sense develops that the process has reached beyond the inner exploration and voicing of subpersonalities. A growing awareness emerges that these inner energy charges, ones I have called subpersonalities, now connect directly with a particular creature in Nature that helps draw them forward. Intuitively, seekers know that this experience is something more than projection onto nature of their inner lives, because an energy charge comes from the outside as well.

These two energies form an alliance that has as its purpose the continuing unfolding of the person and the larger ecology; hence the term *ecology therapy.* Without this alliance and other alliances that will follow, the person is deprived of one of the most powerful transforming energies that exists in our known universe. The data that supports this hypothesis came first to me in my own experience, as we explored earlier, and then from psychotherapists who trained to develop their natural shamanic skills, which I believe are available to a sizeable number of therapists.

Years later Lee had done considerable work on herself. She had been in several psychotherapy processes, completed a graduate program as a psychotherapist, worked in a psychiatric hospital as a therapist, and then established her private practice. After ten years of private practice and well into her forties, she sought an avenue to connect her to the Higher Power. Her work with the twelve-step programs and other recovery processes had awakened in her this desire to connect herself personally and professionally with a Higher Order of Energy. This hunger had led her to training in shamanic ways to augment her work as a person and as a psychotherapist.

After several years of work in this area, she prepared for a vision quest where she would receive a sacred pipe to aid her in her work both as a psychotherapist and a female shaman. As a part of this preparation, she traveled to the big Island of Hawaii to spend time with herself and to be close to the volcanoes, openings into the womb of Mother Earth.

It was a time of the year when the humpback whales were not supposed to be there. As she sat on an isolated beach with her spouse, she spotted a humpback throwing its tail up in the air. Immediately, she recognized that the whale was coming to her as it had at crucial times in her adult life to lead her in some mysterious step of the journey. It had been a gray in the early years and was now a humpback, but its essential whale energy was what mattered.

She had dreamed of whales for some time, but this experience was beyond dreaming. Before her was a whale from beyond her personal boundaries that summoned to the whale inside. At that time she looked backward to see the importance of whale energy in her life, even though she had not had this awareness earlier. She could see that, for twenty years, whales had been important to her, and that this whale energy had been available to her in a teaching and guiding mode. Slowly over the years the whale energy had worked with her inner subpersonalities to open her sensitivity.

At that moment, she could feel the skin of the gray whale she had touched decades earlier on the trip with her mother. The outer whale had now formed an alliance with her inner whale to help her in the pipe-carrying process. If she were carving a totem pole, the whale would be the foundation of her future totems. These first totems are awakeners and don't usually offer much in the way of actual voicing. It is as if the animal world probes to discover if the person can connect enough to pay attention. In Lee's case it was forming an alliance with her inner whale to help her prepare for this important vision quest.

"Maybe," she would laugh later, "the whales have a 'Save the Humans' organization and I was a pet project."

At about this time I—and other therapists in this training experience—began to notice that many clients had routine experiences with animals in their urban areas that they reported in the course of therapy, sometimes as an aside and sometimes with great curiosity. These reports surprised us, because these were not necessarily clients who had shown any interest in Native American ways.

They also surprised us because we had been working under the assumption that visitations of wild animals happened mostly in the wild. We found ourselves and our clients having frequent visitations from wild animals in the densely urban areas of Houston, Albany, New York, Albuquerque, and Seattle, where live different therapists, shamans, and their clients, friends, and colleagues who train with us on this pathway.

These therapeutic alliances with outer and inner animals were taking place usually outside the awareness of both the client and the therapist; nevertheless, the Universal Network seemed to reach out and pull forward subunits of energy in the person, whether the therapist and client paid conscious attention to it or not. As with all growth experiences, though, the transforming work is severely limited if the awareness of the client and therapist is not involved.

At a crucial point in her therapy Betty hesitantly brought up this subject that underlines this part of my working hypothesis: "This may sound a little weird. I had an interesting experience this week. One night last week, I was sitting in the dining room at about 10:00 p.m., reading. I heard something that sounded like a hoarse cricket. I went to the window and opened the drapes and there on the window sill was a baby frog. I looked at him a moment. He looked startled, so I closed the drapes. Maybe the light hurt his eyes? I thought about him several times the next day. What was he doing there? I had this disquieting feeling that he was there for me in some way I couldn't understand.

"Then, the next night, he was there again. I wondered what this was all about. Was he trying to tell me something? Then another part of me reasoned that the window sill would be a logical place to come, because the small amount of light would attract bugs for him to eat.

"I watched him grow. He wasn't afraid of me; he seemed to look at me, too. I don't know why I told you about this. It embarrasses me to tell someone that I have been involved with a frog."

Even though I had had extensive experience both as a psychotherapist and as a pipe carrier by this time, I fumbled with what to do with Betty's story. I was still experimenting with how to respond when these allies from Nature showed up in my life and in the lives of my clients. It all felt strange and at the same time somewhat natural.

I tip-toed between a time in my life when Nature seemed totally unnatural because I was so estranged from its teaching, and my genetic predisposition to be at home in my context. At least, I acknowledged to myself, I was noticing the importance of these creatures when they hopped out onto the stage of my therapy office. It seemed as difficult for her to tell me of this experience as it might have been for her to tell me about an affair. It seemed to her a forbidden subject.

I asked her what she associated with the story, and she recalled an incident as a child where she had watched a tadpole change over a period of time into a frog. Ever since that time she had associated frogs with transformation. Then she remembered an encounter she'd had with a frog while she was walking her dog. She had picked him up out of the street and placed him in her garden.

As she continued to associate, she identified a moment five years before when she had seen two neighborhood boys tossing a frog back and forth. She had rescued the frog and cautioned the boys about respecting other creatures.

Next she talked about how the frogs ate bugs in her garden. "Even though I don't have anything against bugs, they have to be controlled or the plants won't grow. I guess the frog reminds me of the importance of finding some kind of balance in my life."

Then her awareness focused on a remarkable memory that jolted me, because it was so relevant to her progress in therapy.

"Oh, yes, now I remember that I was very good at the standing broad jump when I was a little girl. In the school events I excelled at that, and this frog reminds me of that. That's what frogs do—the standing broad jump. Wow! I haven't thought about being an athlete for a long time."

As you know from our previous discussion, Betty's advertising to the outside world was almost completely feminine. Her dressing had little thrust to it and was dominated by ruffles that hid her body. Her perfume was flowery and devoid of musky odors. We had talked frequently of her need to contact the masculine aspect of herself. However, I had no idea whatsoever that she had been an athlete, since that energy had long been disowned. Now here was a frog calling forward that part of her that could excel at the standing broad jump. What we had not been able to accomplish in the therapy process, he brought forward by sitting on the window sill.

She sat thoughtfully while I mulled over the remarkable presence of her broad-jumping energy. The muscles in her face and arms seemed stronger, as she sat differently on my couch, sinews defined. She breathed more fully as her chest expanded in the posture of an athlete, and I had the sensation that she was preparing for a jump.

She was.

"This whole experience is bringing something back to me, something I've been wanting to talk about for a long time."

Then Betty told of an old wound in her life where she had made a mistake in her profession; it was something for which she could not, at the time, forgive herself. As she poured out the guilt associated with this experience, it was apparent that she was forgiving herself. The frog had formed an alliance with her by pulling forward this part of her that needed cleansing.

At the end of the session, I invited her to continue to reflect on her experience with the frog and see what came up for her. Early the next week, she opened her front door and there was the frog that had been sitting on her window sill.

"At least it looked like the same one; it could have been another. It just looked at me intently, as if it was trying to tell me more and to help me in some way."

These visitations continued on and off for some time as Betty continued the process of cleansing herself of the toxic waste that comes from a severe inner perfectionist and critic. I did not tell her that, in the medicine circle, the frog is seen as the bringer of rain through the singing of his song. I did not tell her that it is the frog in the medicine way that tells us it is time to ask for purifying. Nor did I tell her that it is the frog who asks us to learn to relax and sing the song that calls the thunder. I did not tell her that I hypothesized that the frog came as a representative and agent of universal healing that would help her forgive her past and look forward to a more energetic (thunderous) relationship with her husband.

I did not tell her that, in the Mayan shamanic practice, the shaman fixes the image of a frog in mind, places water in his or her mouth, and sprays it over the body of the seeker to clear away that which hinders change and growth. I did not tell her these things, because she did not need to hear them; she had heard directly from the frog.

He could explain himself well enough, and she was now listening.

ALLIANCES BECOME ADOPTIONS

One way people know they are prepared to embark on a vision quest is that they have grown accustomed to acknowledging these alliances of an inner subpersonality with and outer animal energy. Having carved out the foundations of the totem of unfolding selves by allowing them to have friends in the natural world, seekers become more and more prepared to receive a visitation that will in effect adopt them into the natural world. This adoption symbolizes and actualizes the ongoing recovery of people into their natural context.

The more I work in this area, the more I am convinced that the Larger Ecology is working diligently to overcome the alienation we humans have imposed on ourselves from the Whole. We are the endangered species that the Larger Ecology is seeking to preserve, because we are a significant repository of awareness that the Larger Living System cannot afford to lose. Gregory Bateson (1979), the anthropoligist and researcher into schizophrenia, recognized this point and affirmed that mind and nature form a necessary unity.

As the totem unfolds, the seeker becomes aware that each totem energy balances out another. An animal will come along to call forth an inner energy that is needed to call the person back into balance and harmony. It becomes the task of the aware ego to sit between these various energies on the inner totem pole. A seeker on the pathway receives many names from the different animal encounters over the years. These encounters, usually through vision quests, are interpreted as visitations from the divine source. There are times when one name seems to fit, and other times when another name seems to fit.

From the aware ego position the seeker makes choices about which energy/name is called for in which situation. Slowly, it becomes clear which name fits the whole person, and from the aware ego position the person makes that choice. The names that the person receives from these encounters forms a map of the inner totem of selves; it is not the total map, because not all of the subpersonalities are represented. The major alliances of energies in the person eventually come to be designated by the many names that the person receives over the years.

Some years ago, I discussed this issue of the unfolding totem of selves with a Native American medicine person. In underlining his point, he told me his version of the eight names that the Lakota leader Crazy Horse received. Actually, Crazy Horse did not receive that name, according to the account of the medicine person talking to me, until his eighth vision seeking. Also, the name he received in Lakota is better translated as "Prancing Horse" or "Spirited Horse," but the white culture preferred to translate it as "Crazy Horse."

Each name that a person receives as a result of a vision seeking builds on and helps balance out the name that he received earlier. Lee offers an example of this unfolding totem.

For some twenty years Lee had had the whale as a major totem, even though she had not fully utilized the guidance that whale energy had for her until she encountered the humpback in Hawaii. The whale underlined many different selves that were important to her development. The whale can dive deep into the water, and Lee needed to dive deep into her unconscious to rescue the wounded selves related to the death of her father and of her husband. She had experienced a number of wounds that were so painful that only a whale energy could help her retrieve them. As she fished these bedraggled selves out of the drink and began to nurture and care for them, the whale was not as necessary as it had been before.

In a way her trip to Hawaii was a transition between totem energies. It was as if the whale was telling her that new energies would be coming into her life as a result of the vision seeking, and that whale energy would not be the primary energy for the next leg of her journey. This transition did not mean that whale energy was completely abandoning her, but that the experience of the humpback was making room for something more.

As she drove with supporters to her vision site in northern New Mexico, she looked up to spot a pair of golden eagles circling overhead. As soon as the car stopped, she popped out just in time for one of the golden eagles to bank against the sharply blue July sky. It flashed between her and the sun so that the light streamed through the dark brown feathers in such a way that they turned into a glowing gold, so warm that they burned themselves deep into her soul.

Even though she had not yet reached her site, the vision had begun. The eagle energy was upon her in a powerful form. It consumed her in that moment, just as the eagle had consumed the mouse in the myth. The whale had taken her down into the depths of her unconscious to attend to her inner wounds. Now the eagle was offering to lift her to Father the Sky, where she would experience her spiritual energy in ways she had only dreamed about. The father she had searched for since her eleventh year would take the form of the grandfather energy, the very air on which the eagle glided. Here dwelt the potential of a balance between deep diving and sky soaring.

After several days of fasting and sitting alone on mountain, she received a further vision of the eagle. The pipe carrier who guided her vision fast acknowledged this adoption of her into the eagle clan by giving her the name *Queena en hisse,* Eagle Friend. The *Queena* is from the Komatsi word for "eagle," and the *en hisse* is from the Creek word for "friend."

At that point she thought her vision quest was over, and that she was beginning a vacation in Rocky Mountain National Park. When she arrived there, she told her husband of a strong urge to climb Long's Peak, known by the Utes as one of "The Two Guides." He was reluctant, because the mountain is 14,255 feet high, but he experienced a powerful leadership growing within her that she described to him as "eagle energy." The energy was so strong that he felt compelled to follow her leadership against the advice of his inner conservatives.

Off they went, leaving base camp at 4:30 a.m. After a harrowing experience of climbing hand over foot along a ledge, with fifty-mile-per-hour winds blowing them close to an edge that dropped off fifteen hundred feet, they reached the top. Although her husband was fit and trim, he followed his eagle-possessed spouse to the top with his tongue hanging out. He explained later that his lungs were about to burst, while she moved with ease. She sang an eagle song, the last two hundred feet, that seemed literally to carry her upward to the summit. It was a heart-thumping surge to look 360 degrees for miles and miles.

On the summit, they remembered that the early aboriginals had climbed this very mountain for the purpose of eagle catching. They accomplished this eagle catching by gouging a hole in the rock, covering themselves up, putting meat out for the eagle, and then waiting. When the eagle approached, they would hang on for dear life. If it did not drag them over the precipice, they would be called eagle catchers.

This summit was indeed a fit place for Lee's adoption into the eagle clan to be complete. For those incomparably powerful moments on the peak of this mighty mountain, she was in balance. The whale and the eagle formed a *demo-bo-ko-se,* a sense of harmony and balance, that planted her feet firmly on the rock and her eyes on the blue as the clouds floated by at face level. She would, like all humans, lose this balance, but no power on earth could ever take this experience from her. For these moments, she was not an eagle catcher. She had been caught by the eagle.

TOTEM BALANCING

At this stage in our discussion, I want to point out once again the principal human task: the continual balancing of the organism and its relationship with its context. The human organism oscillates between balance and unbalance. As I pointed out in Chapter 6, we are a constellation of selves in tension.

A central function of the aware ego is the balancing of the energies that pull against each other. When they are in balance, the tension is dynamic and powerful as in a coiled spring. They are in marvelous readiness to relate us creatively to our environment. They flow like the golf swing of a Ben Hogan that sends the ball toward the flag as it is outlined against the beauty of a purple mountain. They take us through the marvelous leap of a Mikhail Baryshnikov in harmony and balance with the rest of the ballet and gravity itself.

The question I keep bringing up for myself and the reader is how to balance the inner energy segments. In Lee's case we can see that the higher being sends messengers and helpers in the animal kingdom to draw out on our inner stages segments of energy that will help balance us. The power self that could numb her feelings came to help Lee at a time when her father died, but it eventually got her out of balance.

The whale energy came to awaken her from a long period of numbness, and after twenty years she was too closely mired to the earth. Through the whale energy, she had grown overly practical. What had originally been a solution had become a problem, an imbalance. Then the eagle came to her to help lift her to the sky, to give her a new kind of balance. On one end of the seesaw was the whale power, so the eagle sat on the other end to help balance her out.

Here are a few other brief examples of this balancing of the inner totem.

In one of his early sweat lodge outings Marv wandered off into the woods. I became concerned about him and found him completely engrossed in watching the forest, in playing with the butterflies, and in touching the flowers. He was so preoccupied in this experience that he had forgotten to come back to camp. The butterflies and flowers entered his vision to help balance out the extreme pusher/worker energy, because Marv was an addict to work. Another shaman present with us at the time said of Marv, "He is one who walks in beauty." The beauty energy had an innocence about it that helped balance out the cynical compulsions of his work energy.

Two years later, Marv went on the vision quest I described earlier where he encountered spider energy. This spider energy drew him into the webs of life where he could observe the raw experience of a spider catching another insect for food. The side of life that had not been present in the beauty of the butterflies and flowers became apparent to him in a balancing way. His innocent wandering energy experienced a balancing tension with his killer instinct.

Another of our pipe carriers, Don I will call him, is a rolfer and lives in New Mexico. His first totem alliance was with deer, and his name at that time was Deer Spirit, a handle that described well his down-to-earth approach to life. His work as a rolfer focused on enabling people to (properly) align their spines with gravity. Two years after his alliance, hawks began showing up in his life, and he ventured out on another vision seeking.

Through his visions and visitations from hawks he received the name *Ay-Yo-Heste,* which translates from the Creek language as "Hawk Person." This totem alliance with the hawk signaled a new turn of his life in moving from the body to the spirit for more balance in his work and relationships. Too, the hawk voices himself clearly. What a soul-searing experience it is to hear the cry of the hawk as it circles the countryside, preparing to dive for prey. The hawk energy was calling Don to voice more that was inside him as a balance to his natural silence. The hawk energy could not control whether he would learn (more directly) to voice his inner world, but the energy could call him to that task.

TOTEM ALLIANCES WITH CURRENT TRIBES

Another dimension of my working hypothesis is that transformation unfolds best for humans in the context of *tribe,* a term I prefer to *community.* Not only do creatures address individuals in context, they also seek to offer energy from the Higher Being to humans drawn into transformational alliances that become known as families, as clans, and then as tribes.

Typically, these tribes will begin with a single individual having a powerful connection with a creature sent from the Higher Being. Then the energy will spread to the family, to a clan, and then to a tribe. It is at this level of interaction that I observe the most powerful forms of transformation. As I indicated earlier, a weakness of psychotherapy is that it does not provide a context for tribal ceremonies. It usually stops at the individual or family level, or, at most, at a small group level.

Crucial to my experience and understanding of tribe is the connection of the people to a tribal totem. Tribes which have lost their experiential base in Nature become organizations and institutions, as surely as marriages that lose their passion and intimacy become dry institutions. The juice for lubrication is lost.

Soon after the gift of the sacred pipe in my life, I drove along a rural highway. Out of the corner of my eye I saw something flash by and hit a bridge. Although it was unusual for me to do so, I stopped my car and backed up to see what it was. I could see it was a bird of some sort, so I opened the car door and cautiously walked over to explore it.

It was a large barred owel, now dead but still warm. It was beautiful, yet I felt sad. I took a few of its feathers and then buried it by the river over which it was flying when it fell to the ground. The burial included my singing a few Native songs I know for such occasions. As I sang, I experienced the presence of the owl:

"I am not ready to cross over yet, because I have come to you to offer my life and guidance for the healing *inipi,* for you and others you know, that now is being formed by *Wakan Tanka,* the Sacred Mystery."

The words were not audible in the usual sense, but rather intuitive. This form of nature talking takes place in a misty zone that is similar to the zone between waking and sleeping. For the next several nights, I dreamed about the owl. Always, the direction of the owl was a guidance for the emerging clan beyond my family. At the next sweat lodge *(inipi),* the two people on whose land we had been gathering told a joint story before I had a chance to relate my experience.

A family of owls had been speaking to them from a tree near their house. They were astounded at how these owls would look at them. As they communed with the owls, they had a sense that they had been adopted by these birds. After they concluded their story, I told the gathering about Judith's and my experience with the owl by the side of the road, and of my dreams. For the next few meetings a wide variety of people in the sweat lodge had owls in their dreams and encountered owls in unusual places, including one participant who encountered an owl in a city park in the middle of Houston. Another had a small owl come to her window for several nights, as if to say something to her.

It now became clear to all of us that owl energy had adopted us as a group. Since owls are known as night eagles, we came to believe that, as a group, we needed to be open to exploring the darker aspects of our hidden energies. We came to experience the guidance of the night eagles in helping us fly into areas of ourselves and others who were brought to our gatherings. We held that owl energy was there to teach us what it meant to be healed through allowing that which lives in the darkness to come to light. With very little effort or explanation, all the people who attended over a long period of time would eventually have experiences with owls, as well as their own personal totems. Thus, our little *inipi* of twenty people or so had its totem, not through a vote but through the owl's adoption of us.

Years later, we experienced as a sweat lodge the receding energy of the owl and the emerging energy of the eagle, as many of us were visited by eagles. These visitations were numerous and astounding to us, because for many it was the first time they had seen eagles in the wild. Many of the sightings were near Houston, where there were very few eagles, while others were on trips in various parts of the North American continent. This eagle energy helped balance the night out with the day. We now were an owl/eagle *inipi,* and our totem balancing as a group was building.

One day as I sat in our *inipi* lodge, sweating, I opened the flap to take in some air. As I did so, the light from outside cast itself on two feathers hanging from the willow branches that acted as the skeleton of the lodge. One was that of a night eagle, an owl, while the other was that of a golden eagle, monarch of the day.

They fluttered, and so did my memory.

At that moment I joined hands with the tow-headed boy who, decades before, had witnessed the flying feathers of conflict between the night eagle and day eagle in the Palo Duro Canyon. Inside me, he seemed to relax as the conflict between inner night and day balanced for one brief moment. Knowing myself, I might be a total jerk on the morrow, out of balance in many ways.

But for that moment the two birds flew together.

TOTEM BALANCING IN THERAPY GROUPS

One psychotherapist receiving training in these shamanic ways noticed almost immediately that his clients had implicit totem animals within, even when they did not consciously know it. As a therapist in a group where many of his clients either did not know about his work as a shaman or were not interested, he discovered some ways to use totem animals to enhance the therapeutic climate of the group in a traditional indoor psychotherapeutic setting.

As the group session began, he noticed that group members were having difficulty making the transition between their usual world and the therapeutic world. To aid in the warm-up, he explained briefly to them about the use of totems in ancient tribes. The group often used a variety of myths to interpret their experiences, so this approach was not unusual. He next asked them to make an inner journey whereby they would meet an inner wild animal. Very quickly, each one of them contacted an inner wild creature. It was as if this animal was just waiting for them to make its acquaintance. The therapist then led them through several sequences of their getting to know the animal better.

Next, he invited them to make the shape of the animal in the form of a sculpture with their bodies. After they had processed this experience, he then asked them to imagine a totem pole in the room, with each of their inner animals being carved into the totem. The discussion following this imagery resulted in rich grist for the group mill in disclosing where they placed all the animals on the totem.

Who was on the bottom? Who was on top? What did they think their imagery meant for themselves and for the group? In what ways was the group out of balance in terms of one type of energy versus another? Several months later this process would be repeated to assess whether the animals were changing, and, if so, to discern if a new animal appeared to help balance.

Although this approach could be seen primarily as an outstanding psychodramatic technique, for me it offers, along with countless other accounts like this one, interesting data supporting the hypothesis that all of us humans have totem creatures ready and available to guide us and help balance us out at any given moment. It is not necessary for the client to adopt a shamanic belief system in order to benefit immeasurably from the totem experience when the psychotherapist can draw easily from awarenesses developed as a shaman. It also illustrates that, for the most part, we ignore this enormous deposit of natural power hidden deep within our psyches.

SHAMANIC TOTEMS

Practicing shamans enter into alliances with creatures for the purpose of co-operating with the transforming process, not only in themselves, but also in others. These creatures will not only help the shamans enter their own unconscious depths (the underworld), but also allows them to journey into the underworld unconsciousness of the person seeking transformation or healing. The shaman works with the outer creature to travel into the seeker's world and to help draw out whatever toxic energy is producing the symptom. At other times the hidden self that lies beneath the surface will not have produced a symptom, but the seeker experiences a kind of pregnancy whereby something inside needs to come forth. Often the seeker will need the shaman to act as a midwife in a situation such as this and will call for help either consciously or unconsciously.

When the shaman responds, this journey is sometimes a long and dangerous one. Before I enter a discussion of this dimension of totem power, I want to comment on how this totem alliance relates to psychotherapy. It is well known in the psychodynamics of psychotherapy that the client enters a relationship with the therapist whereby the therapist's image frequently enters the dreams and fantasies of the client. Sometimes the dream images are obvious, and sometimes they are not. Competent therapists know how to use this energy exchange between client and therapist, known usually as *transference* and *countertransference.*

What is not known by traditional psychotherapy is how to enter the consciousness of a client at a specific time for a specific purpose, usually in response to the call for help from the seeker who will send the message either on a conscious or unconscious pathway. This knowledge lies within the domain of the shaman and is to be used cautiously and with immense respect for the privacy of the seeker. The contract has to be present for this procedure to be accomplished with integrity; the client/seeker needs to know about this process and agree to participate.

Shamans have an alliance covenant with a specific totem creature whereby the creature will aid in entering the collective unconscious arena in the healing process. Sometimes, when they ride with the creature into this underworld, they will do so only to observe what the toxic subunit of energy is in the client. Sometimes, the exploration will include some specific activities, such as working with that subunit in a dialogue to draw it to the surface so that the seeker can enter a dialogue with it in a more aware way.

One of our pipe carriers reported an experience where he supported a fellow seeker during a period of transformation. In order to offer this support in a shamanic way, he slept on the ground and asked his totem animal, a bird, to help him in the other seeker's search. In a trance state he saw himself crawl on the back of the bird and fly to a cave where, together, they walked into the darkness. It was so dark that the pipe carrier could not see, so he relied on the bird to lead him. After a while they came to an opening.

Once outside, the bird led him to a place where he beheld the seeker sitting and struggling with something. As he looked closer, he saw that the seeker was wrestling with a large snake. He felt an urge to move in and help with the wrestling, but the bird told him that their presence was enough to provide energy for the seeker's struggle. At last the snake relented and turned into a friendly energy.

At that point the pipe carrier knew that his task was completed for the moment and that the seeker had come through an important passageway. The bird led him back to the cave, then through it, and finally flew with him on his back to the place where he had originally been asleep. Once there, he could see that his body had remained in place, so he entered and continued his own sleep.

When he awakened, he had the firm conviction that this dreamlike experience was more than a dream. Yet, inexperienced in these ways as he was, he couldn't be sure. He just knew the texture of the experience was different. Later that day he arranged a visit with the seeker. Immediately, when the seeker saw him, she showed him a snake that she had carved out of a limb.

It seems that, the previous day, she had been walking in the woods and had come upon the limb. It had startled her, because she thought it was a snake that was about to harm her. When she saw that it wasn't an actual snake but only appeared as one, she had picked it up and taken it with her. As she recounted the experience, she had had the distinct feeling that the snake had changed into a limb. Later that night, she had felt an urge to carve on the limb, to make it into a snake, and to carry it with her as a strength. She had done this, and planned to keep it as a totem creature in her life.

When she disclosed the snake to the pipe carrier, he could see that it was very similar to what he had seen in his totem journey. His own totem creature, the bird, had wisely helped him stay at a distance so that he could support the transformation of the limb into the snake totem without interfering.

This totem journey represents the work of a shaman who has gained the confidence of his totem creature so that the creature will help him in his work. Sometimes the journeys result in the shaman actually entering the struggle with the seeker with the help of this ally. They join with the seeker to form a stronger alliance until the seeker can travel without them. In this instance the seeker had need of his presence in the background, but not need of an active participation.

What was the transforming significance of this experience? For the seeker it developed that the snake helped draw forth a leadership energy and an ability to advance her work with her own clients. In a psychodynamic sense, this snake energy was the birthing of a new form of her masculine side, as it transformed from the implicit to the explicit. It would help her assume leadership roles with groups that would be apparent to those around her immediately.

I say this experience can be draining and dangerous for the shaman, because it is difficult enough to struggle in one's own unconscious without entering into another's. Yet anyone in a significant relationship does just that. The difference here is that the totem alliance offers a way for protection of both shaman and seeker, and in this case the budding shaman discovered a way to co-operate with the universe that was eminently practical. He was learning how important it is to be with someone when he or she is at a nodal point of transformation and that often the seeker needs only a listening and aware presence.

CONCLUDING THOUGHTS

As the person proceeds through the transforming spiral, several totems of selves develop. As clients begin to disidentify with the primary selves, they can see them as units that no longer have to dominate their lives. They may develop a totem of these selves and call them by names such as the *critic,* the *pusher,* the *judge,* the *pleaser,* and the like. As the transformation continues, hidden selves come into the view of awareness. As this process develops, these selves join the inner totem and have names such as the *jungle cat,* the *sex bomb,* the *gunfighter,* the *soldier,* and the like.

At some point the transforming process will reach a stagnation unless the client becomes a seeker. At this stage the process will oscillate between the office and the outdoors. As the seeker moves outdoors to the world of Nature, it will become apparent that creatures from this outer world are there to adopt the seeker and form alliances for the purpose of the unfolding evolution of Earth and sky, including the individual person. A form of dialogue develops that is beyond the dialogue of the inner parts. This form of nature talking, a recovery of what was lost in childhood, is necessary, because the inner imbalances become so rigid that the person requires energy from the outside to effect the necessary balancing.

Soon these creatures will lead the seeker to join with other seekers in a larger human experience, the tribal totem. In their most powerful forms, these tribal totems interact with the individual totem for the purpose of calling forth hidden subunits of energy that will help in restoring the individual to harmony and balance with the Larger Environment.

The health of any system—individual, family, tribal, or global—is measured in its ability to encourage new subunits of energy to come forward in the person that have a balancing effect on those other subunits that have a tendency to become entrenched in their ways. In this sequence the micrototem balancing becomes a macrototem balancing for the Larger Ecology.

REFERENCES

Bateson, G. (1979). *Mind and nature: A necessary unity.* New York: E.P. Dutton.

Freud, S. (1966). *The basic writings of Sigmund Freud* (A. Brill, Ed.). New York: The Modern Library.

11

Riding the Many Colored Buffalo

When they first entered therapy, Bob and Betty wanted the pain to stop. They wanted to be cured. Reluctantly, they realized their journey with their guide would be much longer than they thought. Then, time didn't matter too much; it was the ride that mattered the most. Then, it was all that mattered. With or without a guide.

Sometimes, riding the buffalo means listening to and embracing the survivor selves, those aspects of ourselves that help us limp along until we catch a beginning vision of ourselves and the universe. As we notice that we are much more than survivors, then we see the red buffalo calf for the first time. He is the many parts of us that are vulnerable. We can't ride him, only follow, because he is so small and shaky.

We alternately experience him and the survivor energy as part of us but not all of us. Then, one day, we notice the white buffalo of awareness, expanding awareness. When this ever-expanding awareness comes into our ego space, then we are riding a mighty buffalo, one that will nourish us. At first even the white buffalo may be small, but it gradually grows larger and larger, until it is a mighty creature, able to lead us to the sacred mountain of the transforming process.

As the journey/process unfolds, we notice the black buffalo of the primitive instincts and other hidden energies. The white buffalo of awareness leads us to him, and, like it or not, we have to ride the black buffalo if we are to continue. Actual animal creatures show up to talk with our inner flows of energy that are often symbolized by nonhuman creatures. These animals are our allies in reaching into the depths for subpersonalities that will not come forward any other way. They are our best links to the Higher Being.

At first it is a wild ride, but it is balanced through the ever-growing awareness of the white buffalo. To ride the black buffalo without first riding the white buffalo is disaster. Or, less metaphorically, to attempt to experience the dark and primitive aspects of ourselves without an aware ego is disaster.

Then, to recall the myth of an earlier chapter, the black buffalo comes to the horizon, bows to the four directions, and disappears. I cannot know all that this image means; its complete meaning is beyond any living person.

However, there are hints. From atop the many colored buffalo the person sees that life is more than doing, more than surviving. That realization leads to an exploration of the vulnerable selves and an expressing of them to the outside world with safe people. *This experience is otherwise known as intimacy.* This intimacy prepares the way for additional communing with the many selves and other people. Or as Bob once put it, "I enjoy just being with myself and with you."

When he said that, I invited him to allow the part of him that just likes to be to sit in another chair. He left his current sitting place (the ego space) and walked over to another space to experience the aspect of him that just is. He sat down and connected himself with heaven and earth, and then started a breathing process that he had learned in previous therapy. We didn't need to talk much, because I could see behind his eyes a BEING *energy.* This energy is the ground of all the selves: it is beneath even the spiritual selves. It is the underlying universal field of energy that holds all the selves together and is the stuff of the universe. It is the unity underneath the many.

This being energy doesn't need to talk very much, for it radiates out, extending the energy field of the individual in such a powerful way that even the most unaware sense something. When this being energy speaks, often its words are simply, "I am." Beyond that is the experience of sitting with the affirmation that this being energy sends forth: "You are." As the two of us sat together, all the pushing, criticizing, pleasing, fighting, fearing, sexing, perfecting, judging, roaring, laughing, hurting, and crying, as well as other forms of doing, quieted down.

They quieted down, not because we did away with them, not because we emptied them, not because we ignored them, not because we resolved them and they went away, not because we were beyond them, but because we were in the habit of listening to and embracing them. They were confident that they had a place in our lives and that we would listen to them with awareness.

By now they knew that we would not always choose to act on their input, but that we would value what they had to say. They also knew that we would not do any of this perfectly. They trusted us enough for a few moments to recede to the background so we could experience the ground of ourselves with each other. These energies within grew more comfortable in connecting with humans and nonhumans alike, so that we knew, not only personally, but also transpersonally, intimacy, the council of voices.

And at that moment we knew what the ride was all about.

Index

Further Resources

William Taegel and Judith Yost, 1215 Bonnie Brae, Houston, TX 77006. Write for information about workshops and presentations on relationships, psychology of selves, voice dialogue, learning experiences in nature and shamanism, participation in sweat lodges and vision quests, tapes, and other writings.

Voices: The Journal of the American Academy of Psychotherapists. Write to 72 Spring St., Dept. 42, New York, NY 10012; or call Toll-free, 1-800-365-7006. This journal is daring in its approach to the human condition and is at the leading edge of articles on therapy and nature.

Ed Tick and Kate Dahlstedt, 78 North Allen St., Albany NY 12203. Write for information about workshops in the spirit of this book, as well as other creative endeavors.

Hal Stone and Sidra Winkleman, 15315 Magnolia Blvd., Suite 404, Sherman Oaks, CA 91403. Write for information about workshops in voice dialogue, relationships, books, and tapes.

Doug Tapp and Carol Agnessens, 1001 Adams, S.E., Albuquerque, NM 87108. Write for information about rolfing, the body, and transformational ceremonies.

Wayne and Linda McCleskey, 6049 44th Ave., NE, Seattle, WA 98115. Write for information about ceremonies in the Seattle area, personal growth, and therapists who are familiar with practices in this book.